*MUSEUMS, SITES,
AND COLLECTIONS
OF GERMANIC CULTURE
IN NORTH AMERICA*

MUSEUMS, SITES, AND COLLECTIONS OF GERMANIC CULTURE IN NORTH AMERICA

An Annotated Directory of German Immigrant Culture in the United States and Canada

Compiled by Margaret Hobbie

Greenwood Press
Westport, Connecticut • London, England

Library of Congress Cataloging in Publication Data

Hobbie, Margaret.
  Museums, sites, and collections of Germanic culture
in North America.

  Bibliography: p.
  Includes indexes.
  1. German Americans—History—Sources. 2. Historic
sites—United States—Directories. 3. Historical
museums—United States—Directories. I. Title.
E184.G3H58   973'.0431   79-6822
ISBN 0-313-22060-3 lib. bdg.

Library of Congress Catalog Card Number: 79-6822
ISBN: 0-313-22060-3

First published in 1980

Greenwood Press
A division of Congressional Information Service, Inc.
51 Riverside Avenue, Westport, Connecticut 06880

Printed in the United States of America

10 9 8 7 6 5 4 3 2 1

CONTENTS

ACKNOWLEDGMENTS

Barbara Bopp suggested the topic of this book to me in 1975. Her idea and the suggestions of Mack Walker, Don Yoder, Norbert Muhlen, and Klaus Wust, all specialists in various aspects of German-American history, led to the compilation of this directory.

The questionnaire used to collect data was developed with the assistance of Carol Rush, Candace Matelic, Donna Rosenstein, Minor Wine Thomas, Bruce Buckley, Rod Roberts, and the Special Libraries Association. More than 220 people answered the questionnaire. Many of them supplemented their answers with brochures, clippings, books, and photographs, and suggested other potential repositories of German-Americana. Several others helped me locate repositories; Adrienne Ash, Scott Swank, and Magnus Einarsson were particularly helpful. Allon Schoener offered invaluable advice on the location of picture collections.

Finally, I am most grateful to Mack Walker and Roger Haydon for their encouragement and assistance.

PREFACE

The study of the history of German immigrants in North America has usually followed the methods of conventional historiography. Research has been based on written sources and has focused on elite culture and outstanding personalities (military and industrial leaders, artists, scientists). This was the emphasis of Albert Faust's *The German Element in the United States* (1909) and other general histories which followed.

Popular history has aroused greater interest among academic historians in recent decades. They are using more local archival sources and historical photographs; oral history projects flourish; and folk culture and popular culture studies have become firmly established in academe.

The study of material culture is a part of this trend in twentieth-century historiography. Scholars have come to realize that patterns in architecture, town planning, design, and decoration are important to our understanding of human behavior and, therefore, human history. In the study of an ethnic group, when the assessment of the group's place in the larger culture is one aim of research, folkways and material culture assume particular importance. The present work makes no such assessment. This is, rather, an attempt to make material culture, and other nonbibliographic sources more readily available to students of German-American and German-Canadian history, through a descriptive listing of locations where such materials can be found.[1] The collections and sites described are divided into three groups. Chapter 1 describes the German-American holdings of 152 museums, historical societies, archives, and libraries in the United States and Canada. These descriptions note objects, historical photographs, ephemera, and historic houses. Chapter 2 abstracts 103 relevant sites from the 1976 edition of *The National Register of Historic Places*. Most of the listed sites are historic houses, but farms, neighborhoods, museum villages, archaeological sites, monuments, and memorials are included as well. Chapter 3 lists 16 European collections which contain useful materials on European antecedents.

The primary emphases of the directory are on material culture and architecture, but historical photographs have been included where the data were readily available, and a few oral history projects are described which in part concern material culture. Throughout, German-Americans are considered in groups rather than as individuals. Emphases have been placed on general characteristics and effects on mainstream culture, rather than the contributions of outstanding individuals.

Like all branches of historiography the study of material culture has limitations that must be taken into account when the criticality of any one object or of the historical collections as a whole is under consideration.[2] In this directory criticality is limited by the factors governing the placement of objects in public collections and the methods by which public collections came to be included in this directory.

The survival of an object depends upon its inherent fragility or strength, the climate in which it was created and used, the amount of use it has undergone, the mobility of its owners, and the value placed on the object by its possessor. This value may be monetary, sentimental, or scholarly and may depend on the object's scarcity or its association with persons or events well known to the possessor. Many objects that have survived time, the elements, a mobile society, and the fluctuations of popular tastes and values, remain inaccessible to the general public.

The creation of public collections and the addition of individual items to such collections are further factors that govern whether an item is included in this directory. A few of the collections described here are fine arts or decorative arts collections. Their holdings are deemed worthy of preservation on aesthetic grounds. The majority of collections in this book, however, may best be described as "local self-commemorative" collections, celebrating the history of a political unit (Cincinnati), an ethnic group (the Germans from Russia), or a religious group (the Missouri Synod of the Lutheran Church). Almost all of these collections show a bias toward wealthier community members, toward outstanding individuals, and toward their pioneer roots. Thus we find within these collections, just as we find in conventional historiographic sources, an overemphasis on certain periods in history and certain levels of culture.

Many German groups by their very nature are not self-commemorative, for example, the Amish, Conservative Mennonites, and Hutterites. These groups do not found collections celebrating themselves—the religious tenets of the Amish and some Mennonites even forbid the taking of photographs. Furthermore, because of their "quaintness" in the eyes of the larger culture, the folkways of these groups tend to be exploited by museum-amusement parks.

Other groups have begun to assemble self-commemorative collections only recently, because of past discrimination against them as Germans. The Germans from Russia, for example, started to form public collections only in the past decade. As a result they are under-represented in this directory. Conversely, the Pennsylvania Germans are over-represented because their history in North America goes back much farther than that of other German groups, and because the long-settled, densely populated areas of the Middle Atlantic and Southern Ontario regions have generated more local museums than have the more recently settled, sparsely populated areas of the Great Plains and the Prairie Provinces.

The creation of public collections ultimately depends upon the willingness of individuals to give, lend, or sell their possessions. Some owners of objects or collections of great historical interest cannot be induced to part with them. As a result, many potentially useful historical materials remain in private hands.

Finally, inclusion of an entry in this directory has depended on the method used to find repositories. About 280 questionnaires were sent to potential repositories during 1978 and 1979. The names of these institutions were selected from other directories, for example, *The Official Museum Directory, Directory of Museums, Art Galleries and Related Institutions,* and *Picture Sources III,* or suggested by subject and area specialists whose advice was solicited by letter. Suggestions were put forth by questionnaire respondents. Newer, smaller museums tend to be less well known to the compilers of directories and to scholars and museum staff, and some fine collections may have been passed over for this reason. In addition, some potentially relevant collections (about 20 percent of those contacted) did not respond to the questionnaire.

NOTES

1. The reader should assume henceforth that "German-American" includes "German-Canadian."

2. Criticality may be defined as the extent to which an object expresses its historical and cultural context.

INTRODUCTION: GERMAN-AMERICAN HISTORY FROM 1683

The term "German-American" in this book indicates a person whose roots are in the German-speaking areas of Europe; who has emigrated, or whose ancestors have emigrated, to the United States or Canada; and who has settled in North America with the intention of remaining here, retaining, however, elements of "Germanness" in life style.

The term includes German-speakers and their descendants from the present-day Germanies, Luxembourg, Austria, and parts of Switzerland, France, and Eastern Europe. It includes distinctively German groups such as the Hutterites and the Amish, as well as German-Americans more closely linked with mainstream North American culture. It includes industrial workers, middle-class tradesmen and professionals in the *Biedermeier* tradition, and the "illustrious emigrés" of the 1930s. It excludes temporary German residents of this continent (such as Karl Bodmer and Thomas Mann), and Americans with German names who have become irrevocably merged in the mainstream (such as Nelson Rockefeller and Dwight D. Eisenhower).

This large, highly diverse immigrant group is united by the German language. It is further distinguished by a number of traits, most of which can be attributed to the conservative nature of German immigration.

For the most part, German immigrants were more prosperous than other ethnic groups when they arrived in North America.[1] They were quick to buy good land (working farms, if possible) and to found businesses soon after settling. They reestablished the institutions of their homeland in their new communities. They seemed to strive for an Old Germany in the New World, for the maintenance of a bourgeois life style that conditions in Europe had rendered impossible. Emigration was more an act of rebellion against the economic, religious, and social upheaval of Europe than a search for new possibilities in America. Even within the American continent this conservative act was repeated with the founding of Hermann, Missouri, by the German Settlement Society of Philadelphia, whose members found the eastern United States "too English."[2]

The comparatively low rate of remigration demonstrates that the Germans were determined to leave Europe (the new, industrial Europe). Although it is impossible to determine the rates of remigration accurately,[3] there are indications that this rate was low for German-speakers in comparison with other Southern and Eastern European ethnic groups who emigrated several decades later.[4] Difficult and expensive transportation made remigration less likely in the early years when the major German immigration to North America occurred. However, it is also highly probable that the Germans stayed in America because they had succeeded in establishing (or reestablishing) the life style they wanted.

The first German Settlement on the North American continent was Germantown, Pennsylvania, founded in 1683 by a group of German Pietists under the leadership of Francis Daniel Pastorius. Although there had been earlier individual German settlers in Amerca, this was the first actual German settlement.

These Pietists, like many other early settlers in America, left Europe because of religious repression. They were followed in the eighteenth century by a number of other religious groups: Moravians, Salzburgers (Austrian Protestants), Dunkards, Mennonites, Amish, and the Harmonists (in 1803). Indeed, the eighteenth-century Germany immigration might be described as "an immigration of groups." The religious groups usually held themselves aloof from the earlier British settlers and created their own communities. These settlements maintained close contact with each other but made no attempt to assimilate into the mainstream Yankee culture. The eventual dispersal of many of the communities was due far more to internal breakdown than to pressures for assimilation.

Germans also arrived singly (many came as redemptioners) and in nonsectarian groups, and exclusively German settlements and areas developed quickly. The eighteenth-century immigrants settled overwhelmingly in Pennsylvania, but also in the Schoharie and Mohawk Valleys in New York, in the Shenandoah Valley, in western North Carolina, and in northern Georgia.

The material culture of the early groups is the most colorful of all the German immigrant groups. Traditional German motifs, different from their English counterparts, were used to decorate books, documents, and even the most mundane household and farm tools. The charm of these artifacts has surely contributed to their careful preservation, and many examples survive. Other German "imports" and innovations of this period were the Conestoga wagon, the Pennsylvania/Kentucky rifle, bank barns, and stoveplates.[5]

Immigration from German-speaking areas, as from all other areas, slowed considerably during the American Revolutionary War (except in the case of Hessian mercenaries, many of whom settled in America after the Treaty of Paris)[6] and the European wars that followed the French Revolution. However, these years mark the first significant movement of Germans into Canada, as

German loyalists from New York and Pennsylvania moved north with other colonists who chose to remain faithful to the Hanoverian king. They were joined by pacifists, and by other Germans who were indifferent to the British-American conflict but were attracted to Canada by cheap, fertile land. German immigration into Canada from the Thirteen Colonies/United States remained steady for several decades and was augmented after 1824 by the arrival of Amish and other Germans coming directly from Europe.

In the years 1816-1817, there was a surge of attempted emigration from Central Europe. Successive years of crop failure had culminated in the disastrous season of 1816. Small farmers and artisans in southeastern Germany also felt the effects of cumulative land fragmentation[7], of technological pressures on the guilds, and of the Napoleonic Wars. Laws against emigration and the difficulties and expense of transportation meant that relatively few Germans were successful in reaching the United States; they were not to come in great numbers until the 1830s. However, this 1816-1817 group foreshadowed the nature of nineteenth-century immigration. Although a few more religious communities were to emigrate to North America (Old Lutherans, Hutterites, "Bimelers," the Community of True Inspiration, the Society of Bethel), the nineteenth-century emigration pattern was largely one of bourgeois families, families who could still (often barely) afford to make the trip, but who feared the encroachments of agricultural and technological pressures upon their way of life. Many of them were assisted by relatives and friends already settled in America and encouraged by favorable reports and letters from earlier immigrants.

By the mid-nineteenth century, German emigrants no longer came primarily from southeastern Germany, but from the central and eastern German lands as well. Many of those who came to Canada and the United States still funneled through the traditional immigration ports of the East, from Halifax to Charleston. Many settled in Pennsylvania, continuing a pattern set one hundred fifty years before; but the opening lands of the Midwest and Texas proved increasingly popular and New Orleans, Galveston, and Indianaola became important German points of entry. The mid-century saw the founding of New Braunfels and Fredericksburg, Texas; New Ulm, Minnesota; and the beginnings of German neighborhoods in larger cities such as Milwaukee, Chicago, St. Louis, and Cincinnati.

In towns and cities the New Americans established bourgeois, home-centered communities complete with the institutions of early nineteenth-century Germany: German-language schools, churches, newspapers, choral groups, bands, and gymnastics clubs. The founding of these institutions coincided with the development of photography, and from this time on photographs became a major source of historical documentation of German-American life and activities. German-Americans also tended to preserve ephemera illustrating their manners and customs (schoolbooks, banners, invitations, music programs, etc.), and collections of such ephemera can be found in many historical societies.

The tendency to reestablish Germany in America continued throughout the nineteenth century, although as the century wore on it was the urban industrial

worker rather than the agricultural worker or small-town craftsman who immi-
grated, settled, and strengthened the newly established German-American
institutions. The cohesiveness and continuity of German-American communities
was intensified by increasing nativist sentiments on the part of Anglo-Americans,
who were at times dismayed by the beer-drinking, Sabbath-breaking, and generally
foreign ways of the Germans.[8]

In spite of nativism (perhaps partly because of it) German immigrants pros-
pered and many became leaders in their fields.[9] German names were prominent
in industry, retailing, the labor movement, and Midwestern journalism and
politics. The great German breweries (Anheuser-Busch, Stroh, Schlitz, Schmidt,
and Pabst amongst them) were established in the mid-nineteenth century.

On the whole, German-American writers wrote in German and were not
well-known outside the German-speaking community. German musicians and
conductors, on the other hand, gained a degree of fame for their establishment
of orchestras and singing societies. This, and their introduction of European
concert artists to American audiences, laid much of the groundwork for the
United States' and Canada's traditions of outstanding regional orchestras and
oratorio societies.

Although the nineteenth century was not typified by the immigration of
religious communities, religion was still a major concern to most German-
Americans. New religions and old flourished together, and German-speakers
were involved in the founding or growth of the Catholic Church's *Central-
Verein*, Reformed Judaism, the Missouri Synod of the Lutheran Church and
other Lutheran branches, B'nai B'rith, the Mennonite Central Committee, the
Moravian Church, the Society for Ethical Culture, the Evangelical and Reformed
Church, the Reformed Church, the German Baptist Brethren, the Amana
Society, and the German Methodist Church.

In politics the Germans only slowly began to take an active part. Again, most
of their activity was directed at their own language group, but gradually they
entered national politics. The most famous German-American statesman was
Carl Schurz, who became an intimate of Lincoln, a Civil War general, ambassa-
dor to Spain, and secretary of the interior. Schurz was the best known of an
unusual group of nineteenth-century immigrants, political refugees from the
1848 populist uprisings in Europe. These intelligent, politically aware immigrants, who settled in the United States in the late 1840s and early 1850s,
exerted an influence on their communities that belied their small numbers.
Many founded newspapers and thus were able to mold and direct the political
views and aspirations of their readers. Others became military leaders and labor
organizers.

In 1873 groups of "Germans from Russia"[10] arrived on the Great Plains.
These immigrants were descendants of German peasants and artisans who had
settled in Russia in the 1770s at the invitation of Catherine the Great (Sophie
von Anhalt-Zerbst). She had granted them dispensation from certain taxes and

from military service for one hundred years. At the end of this time a large number of the Germans (many of them pacifist Mennonites) decided to emigrate rather than to serve in the Czar's forces or to pay taxes.

The Germans from Russia brought with them large chests full of hard red Turkey winter wheat, a strain developed on the Russian steppes. This winter wheat was well suited to the climate of the North American plains and proved to be a major contribution to American agriculture.

The Germans from Russia settled in Kansas, Nebraska, the Dakotas, Manitoba, and eastern Colorado, and made up a major portion of the German stock of the plains. After the passage of the United States' stiff immigration laws in the period following World War I, many Germans from Russia settled in Canada's prairie provinces. The material culture of the Germans from Russia shows Slavic influence, especially in clothing, town plans, and architecture. Currently they are the German-American group with the strongest ethnic identity, brought about by the experience of years of discrimination, first as "Germans" and then as "Russians."

World War I was the grimmest episode in the history of Germans in the United States and Canada. Anti-German sentiments, present in both countries in 1914 when Britain went to war with Germany, took on alarming proportions in 1917 when the United States entered the conflict. German language and culture were suppressed in all areas: the teaching of German in schools was forbidden and German cultural activities were boycotted. In the Midwest there were also reports of lynchings of German-Americans and the ritual slaying of German dogs.[11]

The German population's response to these tragic events was to turn its back on its European roots. Place names and family names were changed: Berlin, Ontario was renamed Kitchener and Germantown, Nebraska became Garland. Schmidt became Smith and Mueller became Miller. German community leaders and ministers (many of whom, in the United States, had supported Germany before 1917) called upon their fellow Germans to buy war bonds and support the war effort in every way. Young men of German birth and descent joined the Canadian and American armed forces. The Germans gave up beer gardens, associations, and other things that distinguished them as Germans.

So drastic were the actions of the Germans, so obvious their desire to prove themselves patriots of their adopted countries, that by 1939 and 1941 the Germans in Canada and the United States were no longer regarded as threats to internal security. (Even the notorious German-American *Bund,* most of whose members were German nationals, failed to attract German-Americans in significant numbers.) There were certainly isolated incidents of discrimination and hostility against German-Americans during the war, but they never approached the scale that had been reached during World War I. Thus, the period between the end of World War I and the mid-1930s was a time of great assimilation. The immigration acts of 1917-1924 restricted immigration severely, so that the existing German population was not fed by as much new blood as it had been in the past. Many Germans who might have emigrated to the United States instead settled in Canada, augmenting its German communities, but the German-Canadians were also rapidly conforming to mainstream culture.

The rise of the German National Socialist Party has been described as a "windfall" for the United States.[12] As early as 1933, hundreds of Central European Jews and dissidents were emigrating. Among them were outstanding scientists, authors, cinema artists, philosophers, composers, and social scientists. Many left the European continent only for the duration of the Nazi regime and returned home as soon as they could after the war. Hundreds of others settled permanently in their lands of refuge, a large proportion of these in the United States. The degree to which they enriched American university, scientific, and cultural life is immeasurable.[13]

Except for two groups—war-brides and displaced persons—post-World War II immigration from German-speaking areas has not been particularly distinctive. Germans today mostly immigrate to the United States and Canada for increased economic and professional opportunities, as do most immigrants to North America.

There is now little attempt on the part of German immigrants to preserve Germany in the New World. Although German-American associations (*Turner* clubs, *Männerchoren,* etc.) abound, they are no longer central to the lives of most German-Americans and German-Canadians. Furthermore, German settlement in North America need no longer be perceived as a final act. Return trips to Europe, for visits or for good, are a relatively simple matter. Indeed, this fact may well account for the more casual attitude toward German-American institutions: there is little need to preserve the ways of the Old World in the New when the Old World is readily accessible.

NOTES

1. Mack Walker, *Germany and the Emigration, 1816-1885* (Cambridge, Mass.: Harvard University Press, 1964), chap. 3.

2. This conservatism is explored in Berton Roueché, "Schoenheit Muss Leiden," *The New Yorker* (February 28, 1977), pp. 37-50.

3. Günter Moltmann, "American-German Return Migration in the Nineteenth and Early Twentieth Centuries," paper delivered at the Annual Meeting of the American Historical Association, 1978.

4. Alfred Vagts, "The Ebb-Tide of Immigration: Germans Returning from America," *American-German Review* (October-November, 1954), pp. 30-33.

5. A selected list of books and articles on German-American material culture is included in the bibliography.

6. Marcus Lee Hansen, *The Atlantic Migration, 1607-1860* (Cambridge, Mass.: Harvard University Press, 1940), p. 54.

7. Ibid., pp. 211-20.

8. Nativism, hyphenism, and assimilation are examined in John A. Hawgood, *The Tragedy of German-America* (New York: G. P. Putnam's Sons, 1940).

9. Most general histories of Germans in America emphasize the achievements of outstanding individuals. The standard general history is still Albert B. Faust, *The German Element in the United States* (New York: Steuben Society of America, 1909, 1927). Of the more recent texts one of the best is La Vern Rippley, *The German-Americans* (Boston: Twayne Publishers, 1976).

10. The Germans from Russia should not be confused with the Dukhobors, or Old Believers, who are Slavs.

11. Rippley, *The German-Americans*, p. 186.

12. Adrienne Ash, "The Great American Windfall: German Emigrés to America, 1930-1945," lecture delivered at the Colorado State Foreign Language Conference, October 15, 1976.

13. The best chronicle of the 1930s emigrés' achievements is Donald Fleming and Bernard Bailyn, *The Intellectual Migration: Europe and America, 1930-60* (Cambridge, Mass.: Harvard University Press, 1969).

MUSEUMS, SITES, AND COLLECTIONS OF GERMANIC CULTURE IN NORTH AMERICA

Chapter I:

COLLECTIONS

SOURCES AND ARRANGEMENT

This chapter consists of descriptive entries of repositories of German-American and German-Canadian material culture. The data were compiled from current editions of The Official Museum Directory, Directory of Museums, Art Galleries and Related Institutions, Picture Sources III, other reference works listed in the bibliography, and from the responses to questionnaires mailed to over 280 potential repositories during 1978 and 1979.

The entries are arranged alphabetically by state or province, then by municipality, then by name of institution. Following the example of The Official Museum Directory, Canadian entries follow United States entries.

SUGGESTIONS FOR RESEARCH

The researcher wishing to visit an institution should always make an appointment, even where "No appointment necessary" is indicated in the entries. Open hours may be changed at short notice and the researcher may find the repository closed. Furthermore, advance notice will give the staff time to prepare registraral records for outside use, retrieve special materials, etc.

It is further recommended that the researcher have at least some knowledge of the topic under study before attempting research in visual resources. It is always advisable to spend some time in the repository's library, should such exist, before examining the museum or photographic collections.

CA1   ACADEMY OF MOTION PICTURE ARTS & SCIENCES
       Margaret Herrick Library

       8949 Wilshire Boulevard
       Beverly Hills, CA 90211
       (213) 278-4313

       Mildred Simpson, Librarian
       Staff: 12 permanent

       Library includes pictorial collections illustrating
       history of the motion picture industry. Still collec-
       tion includes portraits and publicity photos of
       German-speaking immigrants and emigrés connected with
       the motion picture industry in the U. S., e.g.
       Laemmle, Henreid, Dietrich, Lenya, Lang.

       Dates: 1896-present.

       Collection grouped by: production, biography, motion
       picture production, general; library.

       Hours: MTThF 9-5. Appointment recommended for use of
       special collections. Open to anyone with a serious
       interest in motion pictures. No admission or research
       fees.

       Occasionally lends materials. 8"x10" b&w glossy
       prints available at $5.00 each. Copy negatives avail-
       able at $5.00 each.

                          * * *

CA2   CENTER FOR MENNONITE BRETHREN STUDIES

       Fresno Pacific College Library
       1717 South Chestnut Street
       Fresno, CA 93702
       (209) 251-7194

       Rachel Hiebert, Archivist
       Staff: 1 permanent + students; 2 part-time volunteer

       The Center is the official depository for the
       Mennonite Brethren Church records and holds a few
       objects (armaments, musical instruments), 10-20 oral
       history tapes, and several hundred photographs and
       slides, mostly of mission work overseas.

       Dates: 1878-present.

       75% cataloged; 50% photographed; in library.

       Hours: Appointment necessary. Resources available to
       all interested persons. No research fees.

       Does not lend articles.

                          * * *

CA3   LIBRARY OF VEHICLES

       12172 Sheridan Lane
       Garden Grove, CA 92640
       (714) 636-9517
                               California

CA3   (Library of Vehicles)
cont.   W. Everett Miller, Owner
        Staff: 1 permament

        Large collection of color and b&w prints and slides of
        land vehicles including many of Conestoga wagons.
        Expensive but may be well worth it for special
        exhibits.

        Dates: 1691-present.

        1% cataloged; library.

        Hours: By appointment only. Researchers may view
        collection; Mr. Miller does all research. No fee to
        view collection. Research fees $25.00 per hour.

        Photocopies available for study. Photographs and
        pictures lent for special exhibits. Black & white
        and color prints and slides may be made up.

                              * * *

CA4   CALIFORNIA HISTORICAL SOCIETY
        Library

        2090 Jackson Street
        San Francisco, CA 94109
        (415) 567-1848

        Laverne Mau Dicker, Curator of Photographs
        Staff: 12 permanent, 20 volunteer

        Library includes photographs and ephemera illustrative
        of German-American life in San Francisco Bay area.
        Topics covered include Sutter's Mill, Anaheim, New
        Helvetia, street scenes, organizations, festivals,
        schools, portraits, advertising media. Collections
        not cataloged by ethnic group so extensive prior
        research required.

        Dates: 1848-present.

        Library.

        Hours: W-Sat 10-4. No appointment necessary.
        Resources available to anyone. Members may use collec-
        tions at no charge; for others, $1.00 reader's fee,
        50¢ for students.

        Lends only to other museums. Copies of photographs may
        be purchased for research and other non-commercial
        purposes. Reproduction and use fees charged. Schedule
        of fees and conditions for use available from Society.

                              * * *

CT5   YALE UNIVERSITY ART GALLERY

        1111 Chapel Street
        New Haven, CT 06520
        (203) 436-0574

CT5   (Yale University Art Gallery)
cont. Patricia E. Kane, Curator of American Decorative Arts
       Staff: 40 permanent

       Small collection of Pennsylvania German furniture,
       food processing and service articles, housekeeping
       tools, decorative arts.

       Dates: 18th century.

       95% cataloged; 95% photographed; library.

       Hours: T-Sat 10-5; Sun 2-5. Appointment necessary
       for furniture. Anyone may use collections and
       library for research. No admission or research fees.

       Lends items for study and exhibition.

                              * * *

DE6   HENRY FRANCIS duPONT WINTERTHUR MUSEUM

       Winterthur, DE   19735
       (302) 656-8591

       Nancy Goyne Evans, Registrar
       Staff: 200 permanent, 15 volunteer

       Large collection includes bedding, furniture, lighting
       devices, adornments, clothing, toilet articles, food
       processing and service articles, housekeeping tools,
       fractur, decorative arts, toys. Period rooms of
       Pennsylvania German furniture and implements.

       Dates: 1725-1860.

       98% cataloged; 30% photographed; library.

       Hours: Exhibit areas: T-Sat 10-5, Sun 12-4. Office
       hours: M-F 8:30-4:30. Appointment necessary for
       research. Resources available to scholars, graduate
       students, other museum staff, members of the Winterthur
       Guild. Admission fee. No fee for use of library.

       No loans for study. Lends articles for museum
       exhibits. Prints, transparencies, and slides of many
       items exist.

                              * * *

DC7   LIBRARY OF CONGRESS
       Prints and Photographs Division

       Washington, DC   20540
       (202) 426-6394

       Bernard F. Reilly, Curator, Historical Prints
       Mary Ison, Reference Librarian (HABS)
       Staff: very large

       Photographs and other images on many German-American
       topics may be found here; the possibilities are
       almost unlimited for the researcher with time to hunt.

                              Connecticut-Washington, D. C.

DC7   (Library of Congress)
cont.
        Special areas within Prints and Photographs: Historic
        American Buildings Survey (see listing in Index);
        Swann Collection of Caricature and Cartoon; portrait
        collection; lithographs of American cities with large
        German populations; immigration process; business and
        industry; advertising media; manuscript and printed
        fractur.

        Dates: mostly 19th and 20th century.

        Percent cataloged varies with collection; library.

        Hours: M-F 8:30-5. Appointment recommended.
        Resources available to anyone. No admission or
        research fees.

        Some collections lend items; photocopies may be made
        through Library of Congress Photoduplication Service.

        Visual materials on German-Americans can also be
        found in the Motion Picture and Rare Book & Manuscripts
        Divisions of the Library of Congress.

                              * * *

DC8   NATIONAL GALLERY OF ART
        Index of American Design

        Constitution Avenue at Sixth Street, NW
        Washington, DC   20565
        (202) 737-4215

        Peter Davidock, Jr., Registrar
        Staff: 1 permanent (Index)

        Photographs and watercolor renderings of American folk
        art located in various collections in the United
        States. Pennsylvania German examples include furni-
        ture, lighting devices, clothing, food processing and
        service articles, housekeeping tools, other tools,
        fractur, stoveplates, games, toys, containers.

        Dates: 19th century.

        Library.

        Hours: M-F 10-5. Appointment necessary. Open to
        public. No admission or research fees.

        Occasionally lends materials for exhibit. Black &
        white prints exist of some items. Two slideshows
        which use the Pennsylvania German examples from the
        Index of American Design are available for purchase:
        "American Design: The Pennsylvania Germans" (20
        slides, 1972) from the Society for Visual Education,
        1345 Diversey Parkway, Chicago, IL 60614; and
        "Pennsylvania German Folk Art" (50 slides, 1954) from
        Photo Lab, Inc., 3825 Georgia Avenue, NW, Washington,
        DC   20011.

                              * * *

                                        Washington, D. C.

DC9   NATIONAL MUSEUM OF HISTORY AND TECHNOLOGY

14th Street & Constitution Avenue, NW
Washington, DC 20560
(202) 381-5785

Richard E. Ahlborn, Curator of Community Life
(202) 381-5652
Staff: 450 permanent, 100 volunteer

Any one of the Museum's 20 Divisions may have relevant
materials. As a whole the collections include bedding,
furniture, lighting devices, adornments, clothing,
toilet articles, agricultural tools, food processing
and service articles, housekeeping tools, musical
instruments, textileworking tools, clocks, woodworking
tools, other tools, transport, fractur, decorative
arts, games, toys, containers. Contact the Curator of
the appropriate Division: Domestic Life, Community
Life, Textiles, Graphic Arts, Ceramics & Glass, Costume,
Musical Instruments, Numismatics, Military History,
Political History, Postal History, Electricity &
Modern Physics, Mathematics, Mechanisms, Medical
Sciences, Physical Sciences, Extractive Industries,
Mechanical & Civil Engineering, Photographic History,
Transportation.

Dates: mostly 18th & 19th centuries, some 20th century.

90% cataloged; 15% photographed; library.

Hours: Daily except Christmas: Winter 10-5, Summer
10-9. Appointment necessary. Anyone may use resources.
No admission or research fees.

Sometimes lends materials. Prints and slides of many
articles exist.

* * *

IL10 CHICAGO HISTORICAL SOCIETY
Library

North Avenue & Clark Street
Chicago, IL 60614
(312) 642-4600

Larry Viskochil, Curator, Graphics Collection
Staff: 3 permanent (Graphics Collection)

Graphics Collection includes many depictions (historical photographs, advertising media, broadsides, lithographs) of German-American life. Also clothing,
toys in library collection. Collections not cataloged
or arranged according to ethnic group.

Dates: late 18th century-present.

10% cataloged; 90% arranged by subject; library.

Hours: T-Sat 1-4:30 (July & Aug M-F). Appointment
recommended. Researchers high school age or older
welcome. No admission or research fees.

Washington, D. C.-Illinois

IL10   (Chicago Historical Society)

No loans for study; occasional loans for exhibits.

* * *

IL11   GRAUE MILL AND MUSEUM

P. O. Box 293
Hinsdale, IL 60521
(312) 655-2090

Mrs. Chris Meier, Manager
Staff: 9 permanent, 55 volunteer

Mill built, owned, and operated by Frederick Graue
(1819-1892), Hanoverian immigrant (1834). Items in
the museum's collection pertain to the milling
process and to rural American life of the mid-
nineteenth century.

Dates: ca. 1850-1865.

100% cataloged; 0% photographed; no library.

Hours: May-Oct 10-5 daily. Appointment recommended.
Anyone may use resources. Admission fee 50¢.

No loans.

* * *

IN12   FOLKLORE ARCHIVES

504 North Fess Street
Bloomington, IN 47401
(812) 337-3652

Contact "Archivist"
Staff: 7 part-time

Division of the Folklore Institute, Indiana University.

Dubois County (Indiana) Project includes fieldwork
slides (color) of Dubois County, which has a large
German population; topics: buildings, furniture,
adornments, decorative arts. Also about 30 assorted
student papers in general collection may have relevant
materials. Also slides of German-American and Swiss-
American architecture in Clayton County, Iowa, and
Franklin County, Indiana, including bank barns,
central chimney structures.

Dates: 1870-present.

80% cataloged; access to Folklore Collection at
Indiana University Library; archives.

Hours: M-F 9-5, and by appointment. Appointment
recommended. Collections available to all researchers.
No research fees. Most materials have few restrictions
on use within the archives.

Loans unusual. Use of material varies with wishes of
depositor.

* * *

Illinois-Indiana

IN13 ARCHIVES OF THE MENNONITE CHURCH

Goshen College
Goshen, IN 46526
(219) 533-3161 ext. 327

Leonard Gross, Archivist
Staff: 2½ permanent

Large collection of photographs and slides of people
and places within the Mennonite Church; fractur;
Mennonite Central Committee ephemera and photos.

Dates: 19th & 20th centuries.

70% cataloged; library.

Hours: M-F 8-12, 1-5. No appointment necessary.
Resources open to any person with a legitimate
research interest. No admission or research fees.

No loans.

* * *

IN14 MENNONITE HISTORICAL LIBRARY

Goshen College
Goshen, IN 46526
(219) 533-3161

N. P. Springer, Curator
Staff: 2½ permanent

Library collection includes German-American broadsides, historical photographs, and relevant maps.
Museum collection, in storage, includes furniture,
adornments, clothing, toilet articles, agricultural
tools, food processing and service tools, fractur and
similar documents, decorative arts, games, toys,
containers.

Dates: 1681-present.

50% cataloged; few photographed; library.

Hours: M-Sat 8-10, 1-5. No Saturday hours during
college breaks. Appointment recommended, especially
to check on hours and for those researchers with
special questions. Resources open to all researchers.
No admission or research fees.

Loans made occasionally.

* * *

IN15 AMISH ACRES

1600 West Market Street
Nappanee, IN 46550
(219) 773-4188

Richard Pletcher, President
Staff: 100 permanent

IN15   (Amish Acres)
cont.   Living historical farm including restorations and
        reconstructions of dwellings typical of Amish and
        Mennonites in Northern Indiana. Buildings include
        bank barn, house, cidermill, bakeoven, food-drying
        house, outhouse. Other collections include bedding,
        furniture, lighting devices, clothing, agricultural
        tools, food processing and service articles, textile-
        working tools, bibles, land transport.

        Dates: mid-19th century-present.

        Collections not cataloged; partially photographed; no
        library.

        Hours: May-Oct M-Sat 9-8, Sun 11-6; Nov-Apr Sat & Sun
        9-4. No appointment necessary. Admission fee.

        No loans.

                                    * * *

IN16   HISTORIC NEW HARMONY, INC.

        506 Main Street
        P. O. Box 248
        New Harmony, IN   47631
        (812) 682-4488

        Loretta B. Glenn, Director of Public Affairs
        Staff: 60 permanent

        One of three organizations involved with museum
        operations in New Harmony. Most of Historic New Har-
        mony collections in storage awaiting placement.
        Materials relating to early Harmonists include
        bedding, furniture, lighting devices, adornments,
        clothing, toilet articles, agricultural tools, food
        processing and service articles, housekeeping tools,
        musical instruments, textileworking tools, woodworking
        tools, other tools, documents, transport, decorative
        arts, toys, games, containers.

        Dates: 1814-1824.

        Collections inventoried but not yet cataloged or
        photographed; Workingmen's Institute library available
        for research.

        Hours: Daily 9-5 except Christmas and New Year's.
        Write for information on use of materials.

        Cf. NEW HARMONY STATE MEMORIAL, IN17.
            WORKINGMEN'S INSTITUTE LIBRARY AND MUSEUM, IN18.
            OLD ECONOMY VILLAGE, PA79.
            NEW HARMONY HISTORIC DISTRICT, IN159.

                                    * * *

IN17   NEW HARMONY STATE MEMORIAL

P. O. Box 362
New Harmony, IN   47631
(812) 682-3271

Paul Davis, Property Manager
Staff: 2 full-time, 6 part-time

Governed by: Division of Historic Preservation
               Indiana State Museum

An Indiana State Museum site.   State-owned buildings:
Fauntleroy House (1815); Dormitory #2 (ca. 1822);
service barn (reconstruction--exterior reflects
Harmonist design); Opera House, originally Harmonist
Dormitory (1824/1888); reconstructed Harmonist
labyrinth (1820).   Collections include furniture,
agricultural tools, housekeeping tools, textileworking
tools, land transport, decorative arts.

Dates: 1814-1825.

10% cataloged; 10% photographed; Workingmen's Institute library available for research.

Hours: Daily 9-12, 1-5; closed Sunday morning Nov-
Feb.   Resources available to students and other
researchers.   Admission fee of 50¢ charged for
Fauntleroy House and Dormitory #2.

No loans.

Cf. HISTORIC NEW HARMONY, INC., IN16
    WORKINGMEN'S INSTITUTE LIBRARY AND MUSEUM, IN18
    OLD ECONOMY VILLAGE, PA79.
    NEW HARMONY HISTORIC DISTRICT, IN159.

                              * * *

IN18   WORKINGMEN'S INSTITUTE LIBRARY & MUSEUM

West Tavern Street
New Harmony, IN   47631
(812) 682-4806

Mrs. Aline Cook, Head Librarian
Staff: 3 permanent

Harmonist Collection includes a few examples of
furniture, lighting devices, clothing, agricultural
tools, food processing and service articles, musical
instruments, textileworking tools, transport, containers.

Dates: 1804-1840.

0% cataloged; 0% photographed; library.

Hours: Museum T-Sat 10-12, 1:30-4:30; Library T-Sat
10-5.   Appointment necessary for research.   Any
qualified person may use facilities.   Admission fee
50¢ adults, 25¢ children.   No charge to use library.

Rarely lends items.
                                          Indiana

IN18   (Workingmen's Institute Library & Museum)
cont.   Cf. HISTORIC NEW HARMONY, INC., IN16.
            NEW HARMONY STATE MEMORIAL, IN17.
            OLD ECONOMY VILLAGE, PA79.
            NEW HARMONY HISTORIC DISTRICT, IN159.

                            * * *

IA19   MUSEUM OF AMANA HISTORY

        Main Street
        Amana, IA 52203
        (319) 622-3567

        Madeline Roemig, Museum Director
        Staff: 15 part-time

        Museum of the history of the Amana Villages: Amana,
        East Amana, High Amana, Homestead, Little Amana,
        Middle Amana, South Amana, Upper South Amana, and West
        Amana. Museum maintains 1864 residence, 1870 brick
        school house, washhouse/woodshed, and tool shed
        (formerly outhouse). Collections include furniture,
        lighting devices, food processing and service articles,
        agricultural tools, housekeeping equipment, leather-
        working tools, medical equipment, metalworking tools,
        textileworking tools, woodworking tools, decorative
        arts, toys, containers (fine basket collection),
        pottery, historical photographs, lithographs.

        Dates: 1714-present.

        90% cataloged; library.

        Hours: Apr 15-Nov 15: M-Sat 10-5, Sun 12-5. Appoint-
        ment necessary. Facilities may be used by anyone.
        Admission charged for museum. No library use fee.

        Rarely lends items.

        Cf. AMANA VILLAGES, IA162.

                            * * *

IA20   MATHIAS HAM HOUSE

        2241 Lincoln Avenue
        P. O. Box 305
        Dubuque, IA 52001
        (319) 583-2812

        Jerry Enzler, Curator
        Staff: 1 permanent, 4 volunteer

        Affiliated with the Dubuque County Historical Society.

        Twenty-three-room Gothic Revival mansion, former home
        of Mathias Ham. Houses large number of Dubuque
        materials including bedding, furniture, lighting
        devices, adornments, clothing, toilet articles,
        agricultural tools, food processing and service

IA20   (Mathias Ham House)
cont.
articles, housekeeping tools, musical instruments,
woodworking tools, other tools, transport, decorative
arts, toys. About 30% of collection is German-
American but is not cataloged or identified as such,
so much prior research necessary.

Dates: ca. 1820-1950.

90% cataloged; 5% photographed; library.

Hours: 9-5 daily. Appointment recommended for
research. All interested persons may use collections.
Admission $1.00 for collections. No fee to use
library.

Rarely lends articles.

* * *

KS21   MENNONITE HERITAGE COMPLEX

North Poplar Street
Goessel, KS   67053
(316) 367-8177

Orie Richart, Manager
Ben Boese, President
Staff: 1 permanent, 12 volunteer

Complex includes restored Goessel Prep School and old
bank building. Wheat Palace houses exhibit on
Turkey Red Wheat (brought to the United States by
Germans from Russia). Reconstructed Alexanderwohl
Mennonite Immigrant House holds bedding, furniture,
lighting devices, adornments, clothing, toilet articles,
agricultural tools (including German-Russian threshing
stones), food processing and service articles, housekeeping tools, musical instruments, textileworking
tools, woodworking tools, other tools, fractur,
transport, decorative arts, toys, games, containers.

Dates: late 1700's-present.

Cataloging in process; less than 5% photographed;
small library.

Hours: T-Sun 1-5; closed Mondays & holidays.
Appointment recommended. Resources available to
public. Admission and/or research fees adult $1.00,
children 50¢.

Lends articles to nearby institutions. Black & white
and color prints of area structures available for
purchase.

* * *

Iowa-Kansas

KS22   ELLIS COUNTY HISTORICAL SOCIETY

Hays, KS   67601
(913) 625-2448

Staff: 3 permanent, 30 volunteer

Ellis County has a very large German-American population, mostly Russian-Germans from the Volga regions.
Historical Society's Sweetwater Ranch Collection and
photo collection contain many relevant materials.

Dates: ca. 1870-1918.

100% cataloged; 70% photographed; archives.

Hours: MWF 9-5, Sat 1-4. Appointment recommended.
Collections open to public. No admission fees; no
research fees.

Items lent only to exhibits on County heritage.

* * *

KS23   PIONEER ADOBE HOUSE AND MUSEUM (Peter Loewen Adobe
House)

Highway 56 & Ash Street
Hillsboro, KS   67063
(316) 947-3775

Albert Schroeder, Curator
Staff: 1 permanent, 2-4 volunteer

Restored Russian-German Mennonite house (1876) with a
typical "Russian kitchen." Reconstructed barn and
shed house collection of bedding, furniture, lighting
devices, adornments, clothing, toilet articles, agricultural tools, food processing and service articles,
housekeeping tools, leatherworking tools, musical
instruments, textileworking tools, woodworking tools,
fractur or similar documents, land transport,
decorative arts, toys, containers, historical photographs; nineteenth-century windmill and schoolhouse
also under Museum auspices.

Dates: 1850-1950's.

75% cataloged; 15% photographed; no library.

Hours: M-Sat 9-12, 2-5; Sun 2-5. No appointment
necessary. Collections open to public. No
admission fee, but donation requested.

No loans.

National Register Site.

* * *

KS24 McPHERSON MUSEUM

1130 East Euclid
McPherson, KS   67460
(316) 241-5977

Prof. S. M. Dell, Director-Curator
Staff: 6 permanent, 1 volunteer

Collection includes bedding, furniture, lighting
devices, adornments, clothing, toilet articles, agricultural tools, food processing and service articles,
housekeeping tools, musical instruments, textileworking tools, woodworking tools, other tools, fractur,
transport, toys, containers.

Dates: 1890-1950.

100% cataloged; 25% photographed; library.

Hours: T-Sun 1-5; closed Mondays & holidays.
Appointment necessary. Resources available to anyone.
No admission or research fees.

Lends items. Color slides exist of many objects.

* * *

KS25 KAUFMANN MUSEUM

Bethel College
East 27th Street
North Newton, KS   67117
(316) 283-2500

Dee Schmidt
Staff: 1 permanent

Large collection of materials relating to settlement
of area north of Wichita by Germans from Russia,
including furniture, lighting devices, adornments,
clothing, toilet articles, agricultural tools, food
processing and service articles, housekeeping tools,
musical instruments, textileworking tools, woodworking
tools, other tools, land transport, games, toys,
containers.

Dates: ca. 1870-1940.

100% cataloged; mostly photographed; library & archive.

Hours: Collection currently in storage. Appointment
necessary to use collection. No research fee.

Occasionally lends materials for study and exhibit.

* * *

KS26 MENNONITE LIBRARY & ARCHIVE

Bethel College
North Newton, KS   67117
(316) 283-2500

KS26   (Mennonite Library & Archive)
cont.
        John F. Schmidt, Archivist
        Staff: 2 permanent full-time, 6 part-time

        Large archive of documents and pictorial materials
        describing Mennonites from the Black Sea and Volga
        regions who settled in the United States. Photographic
        collection is outstanding. Most photographs are of
        Kansas, especially the Wichita area, but also examples
        of Mennonite farming life in Texas, Iowa, and Washing-
        ton State. Also photographs of the work of the
        Mennonite Central Committee.

        Dates: 1873-present.

        80% cataloged; library.

        Hours: M-F 8-12, 1-5. No appointment necessary. All
        researchers welcome. No admission or research fees.

        Items lent through interlibrary loans.

                              * * *

MD27   MARYLAND HISTORICAL SOCIETY
        Prints and Photographs Department

        201 West Monument Street
        Baltimore, MD 21201
        (301) 685-3750, ext. 77

        Katy Thomsen, Curator of Prints & Photographs
        Staff: 1 permanent, 4 temporary (Department)

        Prints and photographs of Baltimore schools, organiza-
        tions, institutions; Maryland lithographers.

        Dates: 19th & early 20th centuries.

        0% cataloged; library.

        Hours: Prints & Photographs by appointment only;
        library T-Sat 9-4:30. Resources open to public.
        Reader's fee $2.00 for non-members.

        Photoduplication services are available for study and
        publication usage of all Society holdings through the
        Prints and Photographs Department; loans must be
        approved by the Library Committee.

        Maryland Historical Society Gallery may also have
        relevant holdings but these are not cataloged by
        ethnic group.

                              * * *

MD28   CARROLL COUNTY FARM MUSEUM

        500 South Center Street
        Westminster, MD 21157
        (301) 848-7775

MD28   (Carroll County Farm Museum)
cont.
       Cindy Hofferberth, Director
       Staff: 4 permanent full-time; 4 permanent part-time;
            300 volunteers

       Living historical farm with 16 restored structures
       including house, dormitory, 2 barns, 3 sheds, spring-
       house, chicken house, corncrib, smokehouse. Collec-
       tions also include bedding, furniture, lighting
       devices, adornments, clothing, toilet articles,
       agricultural tools, food processing and service
       articles, housekeeping tools, musical instruments,
       textileworking tools, woodworking tools, other tools,
       land transport, decorative arts, games, toys, con-
       tainers. Carroll County was heavily German in the
       nineteenth century and almost all of the collection is
       of German-American origin.

       Dates: ca. 1852-1905.

       100% cataloged; few photographed; library.

       Hours: Sat&Sun 12-5. Appointment necessary.
       Resources open to general public. Admission charged
       for museum, none for library.

       No loans. Prints and slides available of Carroll
       County structures. Slides of bedding, furniture,
       agricultural tools also exist.
                          * * *

MA29   MUSEUM OF FINE ARTS
       M. & M. Karolik Collection

       465 Huntington Avenue
       Boston, MA   02115
       (617) 267-9300

       Michael K. Brown, Curatorial Assistant
       Staff: 400 permanent, 150-200 volunteer (in entire
            museum)

       M. & M. Karolik Collection includes Pennsylvania German
       decorative arts and fractur; also examples of Pennsyl-
       vania German furniture.

       Dates: 1775-1850.

       100% cataloged; 70% photographed; library.

       Hours: T 10-9, W-Sun 10-5, closed Monday. Appointment
       necessary to use department library. Resources
       available to anyone with a serious interest in per-
       tinent topics. Admission fee $1.00. No fee for use
       of library.

       Lends articles for study and exhibit. Color and b&w
       prints exist for furniture, fractur.
                          * * *

                                     Maryland-Massachusetts

MA30   BUSCH-REISINGER MUSEUM

Harvard University
29 Kirkland Street
Cambridge, MA 02138
(617) 495-2338

Charles Haxthausen, Assistant Curator
Staff: 2 permanent

Relevant collections are: Bauhaus Study Archive,
Lyonel Feininger Archive. Study areas: painting,
sculpture, graphic arts, cabinetmaking, ceramics,
furniture, metalwork, photography, theater design,
weaving, wall-painting, typography, design, architecture.

Fine arts library.

Hours: M-Sat 9-5. Appointment necessary for Bauhaus
and Feininger Archives. Resources available to students and scholars. No fees to view collections.
Library use fee if more than six days.

Loans made to special exhibits.

* * *

MI31   GREENFIELD VILLAGE & HENRY FORD MUSEUM

20900 Oakwood
Dearborn, MI 48121
(313) 271-1620

Kenneth M. Wilson, Director, Collections and
Preservation
Staff: 330 permanent, 700-800 summer volunteers

Collections include German-American lighting devices,
Moravian pottery (1790-1830), Pennsylvania-German
pottery (1800-1900), bibles, and fractur (ca. 1800-
1850).

Dates: ca. 1790-1900.

50% cataloged; 50% photographed; library.

Hours: Summer: 9-6 daily, winter: 9-5 daily.
Appointment necessary. Museum "Friends," scholars,
and serious students may use reference library.
Admission fees (separate for Village and Museum):
adults $3.75, children $1.75. No library use fees.

Lends items to other museums. Slides and prints of
pottery and fractur exist.

* * *

MI32   APPEL, JOHN AND SELMA

219 Oakland Drive
East Lansing, MI 48823
(517) 337-1859

MI32   (Appel, John and Selma)
cont. John and Selma Appel
       Staff: 2 permanent

       Ethnic caricatures of immigrants, including Germans
       and "Dutch": postcards, trade cards, lithographs,
       pages from humor magazines.

       Dates: ca. 1860-present.

       Cataloging in process;   65% photographed; personal
       reference collection.

       Hours: By appointment only. Resources available to
       serious students (adults only), publishers, and
       television and film researchers. No admission or
       research fees.

       Materials lent only in unusual circumstances.

                             * * *

MI33   FRANKENMUTH HISTORICAL MUSEUM

       613 South Main Street
       Frankenmuth, MI   48734
       (517) 652-9701

       Carl R. Hansen, Director
       Staff: 4 permanent, 12 volunteer

       Large collection of objects and ephemera relating to
       Bavarian immigrant population of Frankenmuth area,
       including bedding, furniture, lighting devices,
       clothing, adornments, toilet articles, agricultural
       tools, food processing and service articles, house-
       keeping tools, musical instruments, textileworking
       tools, other tools, fractur (rare example), transport,
       decorative arts, games, toys, containers.

       Dates: 1810-present.

       99% cataloged; 5% photographed.

       Hours: T-Sun 9-5. Appointment recommended. Anyone
       may use study facilities. Admission fees: adults
       75¢, children under 12 free. No library use fees.

       Prints and slides of area architecture and of fractur.

                             * * *

MN34   BLUE EARTH COUNTY HISTORICAL SOCIETY MUSEUM

       606 South Broad Street
       Mankato, MN   56001
       (507) 345-4154

       Marcia T. Schuster, Director
       Jeanne D. Kress, Curator for Accessions & Records
       Staff: 3 permanent full-time, 2 part-time,
               2-3 volunteer

MN34   (Blue Earth County Historical Society Museum)
cont.
Materials relating to the history of Blue Earth
County. Small but diverse German-American holdings
include furniture, luggage, armaments, food processing
and service articles, medical equipment, textileworking
tools, woodworking tools, bibles, religious calendars,
land transport, games.

Dates: 1860-1900.

90% cataloged; 0% photographed; archive.

Hours: 1-5 daily except Monday. Appointment not
necessary but recommended. All researchers welcome.
Researchers requested to make donation to Society.

Rarely lends articles.

                          * * *

MN35   BROWN COUNTY HISTORICAL SOCIETY MUSEUM

       27 North Broadway
       New Ulm, MN 56073
       (507) 354-2016

       Paul Klammer, Director and Curator
       Staff: 3 permanent

       Materials illustrating the settlement and history of
       Brown County (New Ulm founded by Turners 1856); over
       65% of collection is German-American. Holdings include
       Melges Bakery Building (1860's), Dahl School; bedding,
       furniture, lighting devices, adornments, clothing,
       toilet articles, agricultural tools, food processing
       and service articles, housekeeping tools; historical
       photographs and ephemera relating to founding of New
       Ulm, education, clubs, churches, etc.; many photo-
       graphs of buildings.

       Dates: 1854-present.

       50% cataloged; few photographed; library.

       Hours: M-Sat 1-5. Appointment recommended for research.
       Resources available to anyone. No admission or research
       fees.

       No loans.

       Cf. MINNESOTA HISTORICAL SOCIETY, MN36.
           FEDERAL POST OFFICE BUILDING, MN176.
           HERMANN MONUMENT, MN177.
           KIESLING HOUSE, MN178.
           MELGES BAKERY, MN179.
           AUGUST SCHELL BREWING COMPANY, MN180.

                          * * *

MN36   MINNESOTA HISTORICAL SOCIETY
       Audio-Visual Library

       690 Cedar Street
       St. Paul, MN 55101
       (612) 296-2489   Minnesota

MN36   (Minnesota Historical Society)
cont.
       Bonnie Wilson, Head of Special Libraries
       Staff: 6 permanent, 1-2 volunteer

       Picture collection contains over 150,000 pictorial
       works with emphasis on Minnesota. "Ethnic groups"
       is a special subject heading. Historical photographs
       of Minnesota German towns (e.g. New Ulm).

       Dates: 1850's-present.

       75% cataloged; 100% photographed; library.

       Hours: M-Sat 8:30-5. No appointment necessary.
       Resources available to anyone. No admission or
       research fees. Research copies made for a nominal
       fee. One-time reproduction fee for photographs for
       commercial use.

       No loans.

                            * * *

MN37   MURPHY'S LANDING
       (A Minnesota Valley Restoration)

       Highway 101
       P. O. Box 275
       Shakopee, MN 55379
       (612) 445-6900

       Cindy Dixon
       Staff: 30 permanent, 35 volunteer

       A multinational living museum reflecting the ethnic
       backgrounds of the Minnesota River Valley: Czech,
       Dakotah, German, Irish, Scandinavian, and Yankee
       traditions are represented. Restored German buildings
       include the Grafenstadt House, Berger timbered cabin,
       bay barn (1855), granary, chicken coop, cowbarn,
       smokehouse (all from Berger farmstead), and Lutheran
       Parochial German School (1867). Collection of appro-
       priate artifacts in process.

       Dates: 1840-1890.

       No library.

       Hours: M-F 8-4. Appointment necessary for research.
       Resources available to public. No admission or
       research fees.

       Cf. SHAKOPEE HISTORIC DISTRICT, MN182.

                            * * *

MN38   CARVER COUNTY HISTORICAL SOCIETY, INC.

       119 Cherry Street
       Waconia, MN 55387
       (612) 442-2062

                                            Minnesota

MN38   (Carver County Historical Society, Inc.)
cont.
Ewald Borgmann, President, Board of Directors
Estelle W. Mueller, Director and Coordinator
Staff: 10 directors, 10 volunteers

Affiliated with the Minnesota Historical Society.

German-American materials include furniture, pipes,
toilet articles, leatherworking tools, medical
equipment, musical instruments, woodworking tools,
transport, games. Society also involved in audio-
visual and oral history projects which may be of
interest.

Dates: 1850-present.

99% cataloged; 60% photographed; library.

Hours: SunTF 1-4:30. Appointment necessary only for
special tour groups. Resources available to all. No
admission fee--donation requested. No library fee.

Lends items for study and exhibit.

* * *

MO39   PERRY COUNTY LUTHERAN HISTORICAL SOCIETY

Star Route
Altenburg, MO 63732
(314) 824-5542

Leonard A. Keuhnart, President
Staff: Volunteers

Affiliated with the Lutheran Church/Missouri Synod.

Altenburg and other parts of Perry County were settled
by Saxon Lutherans in 1839. The Society maintains the
Concordia Log Cabin College (1839) as a museum
housing Saxon furniture, lighting devices, adornments,
clothing, agricultural tools, musical instruments,
textileworking tools, other tools, decorative arts,
toys.

Dates: 19th century.

75-80% cataloged; archival materials photographed;
library.

Hours: Vary. Appointment necessary. Resources
available to any responsible person. No admission or
research fee, but donation requested.

No loans. Black & white prints of structures exist.

* * *

MO40   HISTORIC HERMANN MUSEUM & RIVER ROOM

Fourth & Schiller Streets
P. O. Box 88
Hermann, MO 65041
(314) 486-2017, 486-2718, or 486-2426

MO40   (Historic Hermann Museum & River Room)
cont. Laura Graf, Chairman
       Arthur Schweighaeuser, President
       Staff: 4 permanent, 2 volunteer

       Affiliated with Historic Hermann, Inc.

       Hermann was planned and settled in the 1830's by the
       German Settlement Society of Philadelphia, whose mem-
       bers found the East "too English." Ca. 100 buildings
       remain from early days, many restored and open to
       public; write Historic Hermann (same address) for
       details. Museum & River Room located in the German
       School Building (1871); collections include furniture,
       lighting devices, adornments, clothing, toilet articles,
       agricultural tools, food processing and service arti-
       cles, local pottery, housekeeping tools, musical
       instruments, textileworking tools, woodworking tools,
       other tools, toys. Excellent collection of historical
       photographs: portraits, festivals, organizations.
       Stone Hill Wine Company exhibit.

       Dates: 1865-present.

       80% cataloged; photographing in progress; no library.

       Hours: Apr-Oct 10-5. No appointment necessary except
       for off-hours. Anyone may use collections for research.
       Admission fee for adults 50¢, children 25¢.

       No loans.

       Cf. HISTORICAL SOCIETY OF PENNSYLVANIA, PA102.
           HERMANN HISTORIC DISTRICT, MO185.
           OLD STONE HILL HISTORIC DISTRICT, MO186.

                          * * *

MO41   CONCORDIA HISTORICAL INSTITUTE

       801 DeMun Avenue
       St. Louis, MO 63105
       (314) 721-5934

       Dr. August R. Sueflow, Director
       Rev. Marvin A. Huggins, Reference & Research Assistant
       Staff: 6 permanent, 20 volunteer

       Affiliated with the Lutheran Church/Missouri Synod.

       Collections pertain to the history of German Lutherans
       in Missouri and the history of the Missouri Synod.
       Museum collection includes originals and photographs
       of bedding, furniture, lighting devices, adornments,
       clothing, toilet articles, agricultural tools, food
       processing and service articles, housekeeping tools,
       musical instruments, textileworking tools, woodworking
       tools, other tools, fractur and other documents, trans-
       port, decorative arts, games, toys, containers.
       Historical photographs of buildings.

       Dates: ca. 1800-present.   Missouri

MO41   (Concordia Historical Institute)
cont. 95% cataloged; 5-10% photographed; library.

Hours: M-F 8-5. Appointment helpful. Collections
open to any qualified or responsible person upon
application, explaining project and purpose of research.
No admission or research fees.

Lends materials under certain circumstances. Black &
white prints and color slides exist for many items.

                         * * *

MO42   MISSOURI HISTORICAL SOCIETY

Jefferson Memorial
St. Louis, MO   63112
(314) 361-1424

●Museum

Andrew Van Der Tuin, Curator of Museum
Staff: 19 permanent, volunteers as needed

Collection includes furniture, food processing and
service articles including Missouri German pottery,
clocks, flower stand.

Dates: 1840-1880's.

85% cataloged; 5% photographed; library.

Hours: M-F 9:30-4:45. Appointment necessary.
Resources available to Historical Society members,
institutions and museums, graduate students with letter
from Department Chairman. No admission fees. Fee for
use of library.

Rarely lends articles.

                         - - -

●Pictorial Library.

Gail R. Guidry, Curator of Prints, Paintings,
Drawings & Photographs

Rich assortment of historical photographs, prints,
lithographs, etc., depicting Missouri (especially
St. Louis) German-American organizations, architecture,
brewing industry, churches, schools, festivals;
advertising media.

Dates: 1840-1880's.

15% cataloged; 20% photographed; library.

Hours: M-F 9:30-4:45. Appointment necessary.
Resources available to Historical Society members,
institutions and museum, and graduate students. Use
of Pictorial Library $5.00 per day unless Historical
Society member or representative of other museum.

Rarely lends articles.

                         * * *
                                              Missouri

MO43   EDEN WEBSTER LIBRARIES/EDEN ARCHIVES COLLECTION

Eden Theological Seminary
475 East Lockwood
Webster Groves, MO   63119
(314) 961-3627

Rev. Warren R. Mehl, Librarian
Wilferd Bohley, Archivist
Staff: 1 permanent, 4 volunteer

Extensive collection of photographs of graduates of
the Eden Theological Seminary and their activities;
photographs and lithographs of Evangelical and
Reformed denomination.

Dates: 1904-1924.

Library, archives.

Hours: T&Th 7-3. No appointment necessary. Open to
public. No admission or research fees.

No loans; no material may leave archives.

* * *

NE44   STUHR MUSEUM OF THE PRAIRIE PIONEER

Jct. Highways 281 & 34
R. R. #2
P. O. Box 24
Grand Island, NE   68801
(308) 384-1380

Warren D. Rodgers, Director of Education
Staff: 40 permanent, 65 volunteer

Large complex of restored and reconstructed buildings
moved to 270-acre site. Structures pertaining to
Nebraska Germans are: Windolph House (1860), Lesher
House (1883), Fonda House (1887), Stolley House (1890),
Guild House (1903), Milisen Home (1879), Quillen Houses
(2, 1889), Egger Barn (1870), Meyer Barn (1898),
Paine-Bentley Barn (1880), Quillen Shed, Depot Outhouse
(1895), Schuff Playhouse, Chicken Coop, Lutheran
Church (1888), Oconto Depot (1895), Kenesaw Bank
(1880), Post Office (1860), General Store (1888),
Pioneer Hotel (1886), Barber Shop, Sousa Shoe Shop,
Siebler Blacksmith Shop, Print Shop, Gibbon School
(1880), Township Hall (1884), Vieregg Log Cabin (1858),
Menck Log Cabin (1859), Dan George Log Cabin. Also
transport, agricultural tools.

Dates: 1860-1910.

98% cataloged; 10% photographed; library.

Hours: June 1-Sep 1 M-Sat 9-6, Sun 1-6; Sep 1-June 1
M-Sat 9-5, Sun 1-5. No appointment necessary. Anyone
may use facilities. Admission fees: summer: adults

NE44   (Stuhr Museum of the Prairie Pioneer)
cont. $2.00, students $1.00; off-season: adults $1.00,
       students 50¢; children under 7 free at all times.
       No library use fee.

       Lends articles for study and special exhibits.

                          * * *

NE45   AMERICAN HISTORICAL SOCIETY OF GERMANS FROM RUSSIA

       615 D Street
       Lincoln, NE 68502
       (402) 477-4524

       Ruth Amen, President
       Staff: 5 volunteer

       All materials related to the history of the Germans
       from Russia, especially those who settled in and around
       Lincoln. Included are bedding, furniture, lighting
       devices, adornments, clothing, toilet articles,
       agricultural tools, food processing and service
       articles, housekeeping tools, musical instruments,
       textileworking tools, woodworking tools, other tools,
       fractur or similar documents, decorative arts, games,
       toys, containers; historical photographs.

       Dates: ca. 1870-present.

       95% cataloged; 5% photographed; library.

       Hours: M-F 1-4. Appointment recommended. Resources
       available to AHSGR members and other qualified
       researchers. No admission or research fees.

       No loans.

                          * * *

NE46   NEBRASKA STATE HISTORICAL SOCIETY

       1500 R Street
       Lincoln, NE 68508
       (402) 432-2793

       ●Museum

       Gail Potter, Registrar
       Staff: 76 permanent, 5-7 volunteer

       Small number of examples of bedding, lighting devices,
       adornments, clothing, toilet articles, pipes, carpet
       bag, armaments, food processing and service articles,
       saddle, textileworking tools, woodworking tools,
       fractur and similar documents, bibles, bookmarks,
       communion chalice, containers, and pieces of bagel left
       from immigrant journey. Exhibit on German and Russian-
       German immigrants in Nebraska mounted in 1978.

       Dates: ca. 1800-1900.

       100% cataloged; 5% photographed; library.

                                              Nebraska

NE46   (Nebraska State Historical Society--Museum)
cont.
       Hours: M-Sat 8-5; Sun 1:30-5. Appointment recommended.
       Resources available to the public. No admission or
       research fees.

       Lends items for study and exhibit.

                              - - -

       ●Photographic Collection

       John E. Carter, Curator of Photographs
       Staff: 2 permanent, 1 volunteer

       Excellent collection of ephemera and photographs
       showing lives of German-Russians of the Great Plains,
       especially Nebraska and South Dakota; portraits,
       informal groups, organizations, festivals, agricultural
       scenes; collections with German emphasis are T. F.
       Williams Collection and William F. Urbach Collection.

       Dates: 1890-1935.

       80% cataloged; library.

       Hours: M-F 8-5. No appointment necessary. Resources
       open to general public. No admission or research
       fees.

       No loans; copies available for purchase.

                              * * *

NY47   GERMAN HERITAGE MUSEUM
       Witwe Mehwaldt Haus

       2549 Niagara Road
       Bergholz, NY 14304
       (716) 731-4553

       Eugene Camman, Chairman, Board of Trustees
       Staff: 20 volunteer

       Administered by: Historical Society of North German
                         Settlements in Western New York

       Bergholz was settled by Prussians from Uekermark in
       Brandenburg. Restored Witwe Mehwaldt Haus (half-
       timbered, 1843) holds bedding, furniture, lighting
       devices, adornments, clothing, toilet articles, agri-
       cultural tools, food processing and service articles,
       housekeeping tools, musical instruments, textileworking
       tools, woodworking tools, other tools, decorative
       arts, games, toys, containers. Also pottery and shards
       from Mehwaldt Pottery in Bergholz. Photographic
       collection includes color prints of Mehwaldt pottery
       and historical photographs of Bergholz houses which
       have been destroyed. Society plans to restore second
       half-timbered house in Martinsville, New York.

       Dates: 1843-1900.

NY47   (German Heritage Museum)
cont.
        100% cataloged; 10% photographed; pottery collection
        100% photographed; German-language library being
        developed.

        Hours: Sun 2-5. Appointment necessary for research.
        Resources available to qualified researchers. Donation
        requested for admission and research.

        Black & white prints exist of Mehwaldt Haus and
        destroyed German-American buildings in area. Color
        prints exist of Mehwaldt pottery.

                              * * *

NY48   BUFFALO & ERIE COUNTY HISTORICAL SOCIETY

        25 Nottingham Court
        Buffalo, NY 14216
        (716) 873-9644

        Mrs. Clyde Eller Helfter, Curator of Iconography
        Staff: 41 permanent; 22 volunteer (Society Staff)
                 29 permanent; 18 volunteer (Resources Staff)

        Materials illustrating the history of the City of
        Buffalo and Erie County, New York, which had a large
        and active German-American population in the late
        19th and early 20th centuries. Museum may have rele-
        vant holdings but these are not cataloged by ethnic
        group. Pictorial collection has 25-100 relevant
        illustrations including portraits, street scenes,
        breweries, organizations, and buildings; also litho-
        graphs by Gies & Company; also Mehwaldt pottery from
        Niagara County.

        Dates: late 19th century and early 20th century.

        100% cataloged; 100% photographed or microfilmed;
        library.

        Hours (for research): M-F 10-5, Sat 12-5. Appointment
        recommended. Resources available to any serious
        researcher. $5.00 fee for certain research areas.

        Loans made under special circumstances. Black & white
        prints and color slides of items exist.

                              * * *

NY49   HISTORIC URBAN PLANS

        P. O. Box 276
        Ithaca, NY 14850
        (607) 273-4695

        Prof. John Reps

        Excellent reproductions of plats, plans, and views of
        cities of the world available for purchase at $5-$35
        (mostly ca. $10); includes many American cities with

                                              New York

NY49   (Historic Urban Plans)
cont.
        large German populations. For example, <u>Catalogue #20</u>
        (1978) includes views and maps of Bethlehem, Philadel-
        phia, New Bern, Salem, Savannah, New Ebenezer, Bismarck,
        Sacramento, Cincinnati, and St. Louis.

        Write for catalog and reproduction and rights informa-
        tion.

                              * * *

NY50   FRED STEIN COLLECTION

        115-25 Metropolitan Avenue
        Kew Gardens, NY   11418
        (212) 849-2848

        Mrs. Liselotte Stein
        Staff: 1 permanent

        Photographic portraits of emigrés, political figures,
        actors, etc., including over 500 of Americans of German
        birth or extraction, e.g. Gropius, Dietrich, Tillich,
        Arendt, Einstein.

        Dates: 1934-1967.

        100% cataloged.

        Hours: By appointment only. Resources available to
        anyone with a serious interest. Research fee charged
        after first visit.

        Rents and sells photographs for study and exhibit.

                              * * *

NY51   HERKIMER HOME STATE HISTORIC SITE

        Route 169
        P. O. Box 631
        Little Falls, NY   13365
        (315) 823-0398

        William H. Watkins, Historic Site Manager
        Staff: 9 permanent

        Governed by: NYS Department of Parks & Recreation
                      Division for Historic Preservation

        Home of Nicholas Herkimer, German-American hero of the
        Revolutionary War. Collections include period furni-
        ture, Herkimer family artifacts, Mohawk Valley German
        pieces.

        Dates: 1750-1800.

        Archive.

        Hours: M-Sat 9-5, Sun 1-5. Appointment necessary for
        research. Collections and archive open to public. No
        admission or research fees.

        No loans.

        National Register Site.   New York
                              * * *

NY52   BETTMAN ARCHIVE, INC.

136 East 57th Street
New York, NY 10022
(212) 758-0362

Melvin Gray, President
Manley Stoltzman
Staff: 10 permanent

Large (ca. 4 million items) commercial collection of
pictures on all topics. An expensive but useful
alternative when all else fails or time is short.

Dates: prehistory-present.

Hours: M-F 9-5. Appointment recommended. Qualified
researchers only.

Black & white materials lent for 4 weeks; color transparencies lent for 2 weeks. Reproduction rights fees
charged. The Bettmann Portable Archive (3,600 pictures)
available for purchase.

                              * * *

NY53   BLACK STAR PUBLISHING COMPANY, INC.

450 Park Avenue South
New York, NY 10016
(212) 679-3288

Martin Levick, Photo Librarian
Staff: 5 permanent

Large (over 2 million items) commercial picture collection.

Dates: 1936-present (emphasis on current).

Hours: M-F 9-5. Appointment necessary. Open to
public.

Material loaned for 2 weeks. Reproduction rights fees
charged.

                              * * *

NY54   CULVER PICTURES, INC.

660 First Avenue
New York, NY 10009
(212) 684-5054

Tom Logan
Staff: 7 permanent

Commercial picture collection of over 7 million items.

Dates: prehistory-present.

Hours: M-F 9-5. Appointment recommended. Qualified
researchers only.

Material lent for 30 days. Reproduction rights fees
charged. Picture Guide catalog available for purchase.

                              * * *
                                              New York

NY55   METROPOLITAN MUSEUM OF ART
       American Wing

       Fifth Avenue at 82nd Street
       New York, NY 10028
       (212) 736-2211

       Berry B. Tracy, Curator, American Wing
       Staff: 7 permanent, 4 volunteer

       American Wing collections include examples of German-
       American furniture, food service articles (e.g. Stiegel
       and Amelung glass). Material is there but scattered.

       Dates: 1760-1870.

       100% cataloged; partly photographed; library.

       Hours: M-F 9-5. Appointment necessary. Resources
       available to members of Museum, scholars, and
       researchers/students with proper identification. No
       admission fees. No fees for use of library.

       Lends items only for exhibits with proper security.

       Other branches of the Museum have relevant materials
       (e.g. Print Department--J. R. Burdick Collection for
       advertising media) but these are scattered.

                            * * *

NY56   MUSEUM OF MODERN ART

       11 West 53rd Street
       New York, NY 10019
       (212) 956-6100

       Dr. Ludwig Glaeser, Curator, Mies van der Rohe Archive
       Mary Corliss, Film Stills Archivist
       Charles Silver or Emily Sieger, Film Study Center
       John Szarkowski, Director, Department of Photography
       Staff: very large.

       Many divisions of the Museum have relevant holdings.
       Mies van der Rohe Archive: Bauhaus materials--
       furniture, food service articles, blueprints. Depart-
       ment of Film: Film Study Center and Film Stills
       Archive for immigrant and emigré cinema artists.
       Photograph Collection for artists Steichen, Stieglitz,
       and others.

       Dates: mostly 20th century.

       Percent cataloged and photographed varies with division;
       library.

       Hours: By appointment only for research. Resources
       available to serious students only. No browsers. No
       admission or research fees.

       Some divisions lend materials for exhibits.
                            * * *

                                                New York

NY57   MUSEUM OF THE CITY OF NEW YORK

1220 Fifth Avenue
New York, NY 10029
(212) 534-1672

Albert K. Baragwanath, Senior Curator
Staff: 70 permanent, 35 volunteer

Various sections of the Museum have pertinent holdings.
Theatre & Music Collection--cinema and theater
publicity file, ephemera of German opera in New York;
Print Department--lithographs of the Turnverein and a
Schutzenfest, photographs of ships of German lines;
Museum--dolls.

Dates: mostly 19th century.

75% cataloged; 25% photographed; no library.

Hours: T-Sat 10-5, Sun 1-5, closed Mondays, holidays.
Resources available to anyone doing serious research.
No admission fee.

No loans.

                              * * *

NY58   NEW-YORK HISTORICAL SOCIETY

170 Central Park West
New York, NY 10024
(212) 873-3400

●Museum

Mary Alice Kennedy, Assistant Curator
Staff: 35 permanent, 10 volunteer

Large collection of Pennsylvania German materials
(including Ephrata and Moravian): food processing and
service articles, fractur, decorative arts, toys.

Dates: 19th century.

100% cataloged; 75% photographed; library.

Hours: T-F 11-5, Sat 10-5, Sun 1-5. No appointment
necessary. Resources available to college students,
researchers, scholars. No admission fee. Fee of
$1.00 per day for non-members' use of library.

Lends articles for special exhibits. Black & white
prints and color transparencies exist for many items.

                              - - -

●Print Room

Wendy Shadwell, Curator of Prints
Staff: 2 permanent

Best source for New York City German materials.
Historical photographs, ephemera, and advertising
media (Landauer Collection), illustrating German-

                                              New York

NY58   (New-York Historical Society--Print Room)
cont.
American churches, buildings, businesses, organizations;
fractur. Many photographs of Pennsylvania German
materials in other museum collections, especially
decorative arts and fractur.

Dates: 1700-1940.

50% cataloged; 25% photographed; library.

Hours: T-Sat 10-5. Appointment necessary for certain
special collections. Resources available to adults.
No admission fee. Library fee for non-members.

Occasionally lends materials to other institutions for
exhibit.

* * *

NY59   OLD LUTHERAN PARSONAGE

P. O. Box 556
Schoharie, NY 12157
(518) 295-7505

Staff: volunteer

Administered by: Schoharie Colonial Heritage
                  Association

Restored parsonage built 1743; oldest structure in
Schoharie County. Wattle and daub. Presently fitted
with borrowed furniture and other articles appropriate
to period.

Dates: 18th century.

Not yet cataloged or photographed; no library.

Hours: June-Oct Sat & Sun 9-5. No appointment
necessary. Resources available to public. Admission
fee adults $1.00, children 50¢.

No loans.

National Register Site.

* * *

NY60   OLD STONE FORT MUSEUM & WILLIAM W. BADGLEY HISTORICAL
       MUSEUM

Schoharie, NY 12157
(518) 295-7192

Col. William H. Seeger, Director
Staff: 2 permanent full-time, 6 part-time

Affiliated with the Schoharie County Historical Society.

The Schoharie Valley was settled by Palatines in 1712.
The Old Stone Fort was originally a church, erected by
the Reformed Protestant High Dutch Church Society in
1772. German materials housed there and in the Badgley

New York

NY60   (Old Stone Fort Museum & William W. Badgley Historical
        Museum)

        Museum include bedding, furniture, lighting devices,
        adornments, clothing, toilet articles, agricultural
        tools, food processing and service articles, house-
        keeping tools, musical instruments, textileworking
        tools, woodworking tools, other tools, fractur, games,
        toys, containers. The Historical Society also main-
        tains a restored 1740 Palatine wattle and daub house.

        Dates: 1730-1870.

        0% cataloged; 0% photographed; library.

        Hours: June-Aug daily 10-5; May, Sep, Oct T-Sun 10-5;
        closed Nov-Apr. No appointment necessary. Resources
        open to public. Admission fee adult $1.00. No
        research fees.

        No loans.

                              * * *

NC61   HISTORIC SALISBURY FOUNDATION

        226 South Jackson Street
        Salisbury, NC 28144
        (704) 636-1502

        Clyde Overcash, Custodian
        Ed Clement, President
        Staff: volunteer

        Salisbury was settled in the 18th century by Rhine-
        landers and Pennsylvania Germans. Historic Salisbury
        is itself small (furniture, decorative arts), but
        write there for information on other places of
        interest in Salisbury and Rowan County. Many 18th- and
        19th-century buildings including churches, houses,
        bakeovens, log barns, kitchens, corncribs, shops,
        schoolhouse.

        Dates: 18th and 19th centuries.

        0% cataloged; 0% photographed; no library, but Rowan
        Public Library History Room available.

        Hours: Sun 2-5, or by appointment. Resources available
        to anyone. Admission fees adults $1.00, children 50¢.

        Lends items for study and exhibit.

                              * * *

NC62   ROWAN MUSEUM, INC.

        114 South Jackson Street
        P. O. Box 439
        Salisbury, NC 28144
        (704) 633-5946

        Mrs. Gettys Guille, Director
        Staff: 6 hostesses, 2 volunteers

                                   New York-North Carolina

NC62 (Rowan Museum, Inc.)
cont.
      Museum maintains restored Old Stone House at Granite
      Quarry, built by Pennsylvania German settler 1758-66;
      collections at main museum (Maxwell Chambers House)
      include bedding, furniture, lighting devices, food
      processing and service articles, textileworking tools.

      Dates: 18th century, nothing later than 1810.

      0% cataloged; 0% photographed; no library, but Rowan
      Public Library has local history collection.

      Hours: Winter: T-Sun 2-5; Summer: WSat&Sun 2-5.
      No appointment necessary to view or use collections.
      Resources available to public. Admission 50¢,
      includes guided tour.

      No loans.

      Cf. MICHAEL BRAUN HOUSE, NC197.

                          * * *

NC63 HISTORIC BETHABARA

      2147 Bethabara Road
      Winston-Salem, NC   27108

      (919) 924-8191 or 727-2063

      Ann Cross, Director
      Staff: 2 permanent full-time, 11 part-time

      Affiliated with the Moravian Church.

      Museum village of reconstructed and restored buildings
      housing collections dealing with Moravians in Southern
      Province. (Bethabara was the first Moravian settle-
      ment in North Carolina, 1753.) Restored buildings
      include Gemein Haus (1788), Brewer's House (1803),
      Potter's House (1782). Also many reconstructed
      18th- and 19th century buildings; also archaeological
      sites. Collections include original and reconstructed
      bedding, furniture, lighting devices, agricultural
      tools, food processing and service tools, housekeeping
      tools, textileworking tools, other tools, decorative
      arts, containers; outstanding examples of Moravian
      pottery.

      Dates: 1750-1800.

      100% cataloged; 75% photographed.

      Hours: Easter-Nov 30 M-F 9:30-4:30; Sat&Sun 1:30-4:30;
      closed winter. Collections may be used for research
      only by staff. No admission fees for museum.

      No loans. Slides exist for most articles.

      Cf. BETHABARA MORAVIAN CHURCH, NC201.

                          * * *

                                            North Carolina

NC64   MORAVIAN MUSIC FOUNDATION

20 Cascade Avenue
Winston-Salem, NC   27108
(919) 725-0651

Karl Kroeger, Director
Staff: 7 permanent (+5 in Bethlehem, Pa.)

An archive of early American Moravian music including
manuscripts, song books, song sheets, hymnals; also
works on music history and theory that relate to or
contrast with the music of the Moravian Church. A
few musical instruments, but larger collections
exist in Bethlehem.

Dates: 1740-1870.

80% cataloged; 20-30% photographed; library.

Hours: M-F 8:30-12, 1-4:30. Appointment recommended.
Resources available to legitimate researchers. No
admission or research fees.

Absolutely no loans.

Cf. ARCHIVES OF THE MORAVIAN CHURCH, PA82.

* * *

NC65   OLD SALEM, INC.

600 South Main Street
Drawer F., Salem Station
Winston-Salem, NC   27108
(919) 723-3688

Paula Welshimer, Curator
Staff: 34 permanent full-time, 140 part-time

Salem was settled by Moravians in 1766. There are
many restored private homes in the city in addition to
those maintained by Old Salem: Single Brothers House
(1769, 1786), John Vogler House (1819), Salem Tavern
(1784) and barn, Miksch Tobacco Shop (1771), Winkler
Bakery (1880), Schultz Shoemaker Shop (1827), Boys
School (1794), Market-Fire House (1803). Collections
include bedding, furniture, lighting devices, adornments, clothing, toilet articles, agricultural tools,
food processing and service articles, housekeeping
tools, musical instruments, textileworking tools,
woodworking tools, firefighting equipment, other
tools, transport, fractur or similar documents, decorative arts, games, toys, containers.

Dates: 1766-1840.

100% cataloged; 70% photographed; library.

Hours: M-Sat 9:30-4:30, Sun 1:30-4:30. Appointment
necessary. Resources available to anyone with a

NC65   (Old Salem, Inc.)
cont.
        particular interest or students/scholars. No admission
        or research fees for researchers. General admission
        fee for all Old Salem restored buildings adults $3.50,
        students $1.00.

        Occasionally lends items for exhibit. Prints and
        slides of many objects are available for purchase.
        Those for which there are no existing slides or nega-
        tives may be photographed upon request with an addi-
        tional set-up fee.

        Cf. OLD SALEM HISTORIC DISTRICT, NC202.
            SALEM TAVERN, NC203.
            SINGLE BROTHERS' HOUSE, NC204.
            ZEVELY HOUSE, NC205.

                                * * *

ND66   STATE HISTORICAL SOCIETY OF NORTH DAKOTA

        Liberty Memorial Building
        Bismarck, ND 58501
        (701) 224-2666

        Frank E. Vyzralek, Archivist
        William Leingang, Curator of Photography
        Larry Remele, Director of Education & Interpretation
        Norman Paulson, Curator of Museums
        Staff: 6 permanent

        Museum collection includes Russian-German clothing
        and tools. Photograph Collection includes relevant
        historical photographs. Collections are not broken
        down by ethnic group.

        Dates: 1870-1920.

        100% cataloged; library.

        Hours: M-F 8-12, 1-5. Appointment necessary to
        examine museum items; no appointment for library.
        Resources available to anyone. No admission or research
        fees.

        No loans.

                                * * *

ND67   GEOGRAPHICAL CENTER MUSEUM
        Stumpp Exhibition Hall

        U. S. Highway 2
        Rugby, ND 58368
        (701) 776-6414

        Mrs. Irene Friedrich, American Historical Society of
                              Germans from Russia
                              Heart of America Chapter
                              313 Third Avenue SW
                              Rugby, ND 58368

ND67   (Geographical Center Museum)
cont.
       Staff: 5 volunteer (Exhibition Hall)

       Pioneer village museum of 15-20 buildings with
       collections depicting the lives of early settlers of
       the Rugby area. Stumpp Exhibition Hall is a restored
       building, typical residence of the early Germans from
       Russia who settled in the Dakotas. Collection includes
       bedding, furniture, lighting devices, adornments,
       clothing, agricultural tools, food processing and
       service articles, housekeeping tools, fractur or
       similar documents, decorative arts, toys, containers.

       Dates: ca. 1875-1920.

       10% cataloged; 10% photographed; library in museum;
       also Heart of America Library in Rugby.

       House: May-Sep 9-5. No appointment necessary. Open
       to public. Admission charged to Geographical Center
       Museum. No loans.

                              * * *

OH68   SWISS COMMUNITY HISTORICAL SOCIETY MUSEUM

       P. O. Box 5
       Bluffton, OH   45817
       (419) 384-3661

       Dr. Delbert Gratz, President
       Staff: volunteers as needed

       Christian Schumacher House (1847) houses bedding,
       furniture, lighting devices, clothing, adornments,
       agricultural tools, food processing and service
       articles, housekeeping tools, musical instruments,
       textileworking tools, woodworking tools, fractur,
       transport, decorative arts, games, toys, containers.

       Dates: 1840's-1920's.

       75% cataloged; 5% photographed; library (unorganized).

       Hours: By appointment only. Resources available to
       anyone engaged in serious research. No admission or
       research fees, but donation requested.

       Lends articles occasionally upon application to Board.
       Slides and b&w prints exist of Schumacher House and
       tool shed on property.

                              * * *

OH69   CINCINNATI HISTORICAL SOCIETY

       Eden Park
       Cincinnati, OH   45202
       (513) 241-4622

OH69   (Cincinnati Historical Society)
cont.
       Laura L. Chace, Chief Librarian
       Staff: 21 permanent, 20 volunteer

       ●Library

       Outstanding collection of photographs and ephemera
       describing the lives of Cincinnati's substantial German-
       American population. Topics include brewing and meat-
       packing industries, family portraits, German-American
       soldiers in Europe in World War I, clubs, festivals,
       restaurants; fractur.

       Dates: 1830-1965.

       50% cataloged; library.

       Hours: M-F 8:30-4:30, Sat 9-4 (except June-Aug). No
       appointment necessary for research. Resources available
       to public. No admission or research fees.

       Items lent for exhibits.

                            - - -

       ●Louis & Ida E. Nippert Collection of German Methodism

       Items (manuscripts, printed matter, photographs, and
       over 100 objects) relating to the history of German
       Methodism in the United States. Objects include
       ceremonial artifacts (communion vessels, chalices,
       medals), personal gear, and clothing.

       Dates: mostly 19th century.

       100% cataloged; library.

       Hours: M-F 8:30-4:30, Sat 9-4 (except June-Aug).
       Appointment necessary for research. Resources open to
       public. No admission or research fees.

                            * * *

OH70   AMERICAN JEWISH ARCHIVES

       Jewish Institute of Religion
       Hebrew Union College
       Clifton Avenue
       Cincinnati, OH 45220
       (513) 221-1875

       Fannie Zelcer, Archivist
       Staff: 8 permanent

       Archive of the history of Jews in America. Historical
       photographs and ephemera relating to several prominent
       German-Jewish Americans, e.g. Isaac Meyer Wise,
       Steinmetz, Frankfurter, Rosenwald, Jacobi.

       Dates: 1841-1920.

       100% cataloged; archives.

                                              Ohio

OH70   (American Jewish Archives)
cont.
       Hours: M-F 8:30-5. No appointment necessary.
       Resources available to all serious researchers. No
       admission or research fees.

       No loans.

                              * * *

OH71   WESTERN RESERVE HISTORICAL SOCIETY
       Library

       10825 East Boulevard
       Cleveland, OH 44106
       (216) 721-5722

       John J. Grabowski, Associate Curator of Manuscripts

       Fine collection of historical photographs of Cleveland
       area's German community including portraits, business
       and industry, churches, organizations, brewing industry.

       Dates: 19th and 20th centuries.

       Well-cataloged; library.

       Hours: By appointment only. Resources open to public.
       No admission or research fees.

       Contact Society for borrowing and reproduction informa-
       tion. Heckewelder Map (1796) has been published.

                              * * *

OH72   OHIO HISTORICAL CENTER

       I-71 & 17th Avenue
       Columbus, OH 43211
       (614) 466-2060

       Arlene J. Peterson, Audiovisual Archivist
       Donald A. Hutslar, Associate Curator
       Staff: very large

       Affiliated with the Ohio Historical Society.

       Historical photographs of brewing industry in Ohio,
       and the settlements of Zoar and Schoenbrunn. Fractur
       located in the History Department.

       Dates: 1880-1950.

       50% cataloged; library.

       Hours: M-Sat 9-5, except holidays. No appointment
       necessary. Resources available to public. No
       admission or library use fees.

       No loans. Photographic reproductions available for a
       fee.

       Cf. SCHOENBRUNN VILLAGE STATE MEMORIAL, OH75.
            ZOAR STATE MEMORIAL, OH76.

                              * * *

                                              Ohio

OH73   AU GLAIZE VILLAGE

Krouse Road
P. O. Box 801
Defiance, OH   43512
(419) 784-0107

Walter Font, Curator
Staff: 1 permanent, 15 volunteer

Administered by the Defiance County Historical Society.

A museum village (begun in 1966) of 17 restored and
reconstructed buildings illustrating early 19th-century
rural life in northwest Ohio. The area had many German
settlers and German-American materials are scattered
throughout the buildings. Of probable German origin
are the Kieffer Log Cabin, Arp's Century Log House,
Jacob Myers General Store and Cider Mill, and the
Minsel Barber Shop. Collections also include German
bibles, communal set and baptismal font.

Hours: June-Aug, Sun 1-5, Wed-Sat 10-5; Sep & Oct
Sat&Sun 1-5. Closed Oct 31-Memorial Day. Appointment
necessary to do research. Anyone with a legitimate
purpose may use research facilities. Admission fees:
adults $1.50, students 6-16 and senior citizens 75¢,
children under 6 free.

No loans.

                          * * *

OH74   NEW BREMEN HISTORIC ASSOCIATION MUSEUM

120-122 North Main Street
New Bremen, OH   45869
no phone

Rosemary Heitkamp, Curator
Staff: 1 permanent, 15 volunteer

New Bremen was settled by Germans and Americans of
German descent in 1833. Museum (only recently started)
is housed in early (1837) frame house. Collection
made up of objects lent by descendents of early
settlers, slides and prints of over 200 local buildings,
and ice-cutting equipment from the Miami & Erie Canal,
on which many early settlers were employed.

Dates: late 1800's-early 1900's.

100% cataloged; library.

Hours: T&Th 8-5. Appointment necessary. Anyone may
use research facilities. No admission fee, donation
requested.

Lends items for study and special exhibits.

                          * * *

                                                  Ohio

OH75   SCHOENBRUNN VILLAGE STATE MEMORIAL

        U. S. Route 250
        New Philadelphia, OH   44663
        (216) 343-9711

        Governed by the Ohio Historical Society.

        Restoration of 19 log structures of Ohio's first
        settlement, the Moravian Indian Mission (1772).

        Dates: 18th century.

        Ohio Historical Society library.

        Hours: Apr-Oct daily 10-6. No appointment necessary.
        Resources available to public. Admission fees adult
        $1.00, children 50¢, free if with parent. Ohio
        Historical Society members free.

        Cf. OHIO HISTORICAL CENTER, OH72.

                                * * *

OH76   ZOAR STATE MEMORIAL

        P. O. Box 404
        Zoar, OH   44697
        (216) 874-3211

        Kathleen M. Fernandez, Curator
        Staff: 12 permanent (in season)

        Governed by the Ohio Historical Society.

        Communal village established 1817 by 300 Separatists
        from Württemburg; dissolved 1898. Ohio Historical
        Society owns Bimeler Museum (1869--now Visitors'
        Orientation Center); Number One House (1835--built as
        dormitory); barn (1874--not open to public); Sewing
        House (1835?--open by appointment); bakery (1845);
        tinshop (1825--restoration); wagon shop (ca. 1835--
        reconstruction); blacksmith shop (ca. 1835--reconstruc-
        tion); garden house (1840); geometric pleasure garden.
        Collections include bedding, furniture, lighting
        devices, clothing, agricultural tools, food processing
        and service articles, housekeeping tools, musical
        instruments, textileworking tools, woodworking tools,
        other tools, transport, decorative arts, toys. Other
        buildings and collections in Zoar may be relevant but
        are privately owned.

        Dates: 1817-1898, some later.

        Collection inventoried; 0% photographed; Ohio Histori-
        cal Society library.

        Hours: Apr-June 14, Labor Day-Oct 31 9:30-5; June 15-
        Labor Day 10-6; winter by appointment. No appointment
        necessary except in winter. Anyone may use resources.
        Admission adults $1.00, children 50¢. No research fees.

                                                          Ohio

OH76   (Zoar State Memorial)
cont.
       Lends items in special circumstances. Prints and
       slides of items in the collection may be made; write
       for fee schedule.

       National Register Site.
       Historic American Buildings Survey.

       Cf. OHIO HISTORICAL CENTER, OH72.

                            * * *

OR77   OREGON HISTORICAL SOCIETY
       Photograph Collection

       1230 S. W. Park Avenue
       Portland, OR 97205
       (503) 222-1741

       Susan Seyl, Photographs Librarian
       Staff: 4 permanent, 25-30 volunteer (Collection)

       Historical photographs of German settlers in the
       Northwest. When present computer-assisted cataloging
       project is completed, photographs will be cross-
       referenced to immigration and ethnic groups by specific
       names of groups.

       Dates: 1850-present.

       95% cataloged; library.

       Hours: M-Sat 10-4:45. No appointment necessary.
       Resources available to adults and to students by
       special arrangement. No admission or research fees.

       No loans. Photo reproductions available; write for
       price schedule.

                            * * *

PA78   LEHIGH COUNTY HISTORICAL SOCIETY

       414 Walnut Street
       Allentown, PA 18102
       (215) 435-1074

       John K. Heyl, President
       Staff: 3 permanent, 3 volunteer

       Society maintains three 18th-century houses, barn
       (19th century), shed (19th century); collections include
       bedding, furniture, lighting devices, agricultural
       tools, food processing and service articles, house-
       keeping tools, musical instruments, textileworking
       tools, woodworking tools, transport, fractur, decora-
       tive arts, toys, containers.

       Dates: 18th-20th centuries.

       80% cataloged; library.

PA78   (Lehigh County Historical Society)
cont.
        Hours: T-F 10-12, 1-4. No appointment necessary.
        Anyone may use library and collections. No admission
        or research fees.

        No loans.

                              * * *

PA79   OLD ECONOMY VILLAGE

        14th & Church Streets
        Ambridge, PA 15003
        (412) 266-4500

        Daniel B. Reibel, Curator
        Staff: 21 permanent, 300 volunteer

        Governed by the Pennsylvania Historical & Museum
        Commission.

        The principal location of Harmonist (Rappite) materials
        comprising 17 restored and reconstructed Harmonist
        structures including four houses (1824-31), one barn,
        two sheds, two shops, two churches (off grounds),
        one school (off grounds), one granary; blueprints.
        Collections include bedding, furniture, lighting
        devices, adornments, clothing, toilet articles,
        agricultural tools, food processing and service
        articles, housekeeping tools, musical instruments,
        textileworking tools, woodworking tools, other tools,
        transport, advertising media, fractur, decorative
        arts, containers; historical photographs; grotto (1826).

        Dates: 19th century.

        90% cataloged; 1% photographed; library.

        Hours: M-Sat 8:30-5, Sun 12-5. Appointment necessary.
        Resources available to competent researchers with a
        specific goal. No admission or library use fees for
        researchers; admission charged for tourists.

        Occasionally lends items for study and exhibit. Ca.
        100 slides exist of Harmonist structures.

        National Register Site.
        National Historic Landmark.

        Cf. HISTORIC NEW HARMONY, INC., IN16.
            NEW HARMONY STATE MEMORIAL, IN17.
            WORKINGMEN'S INSTITUTE LIBRARY & MUSEUM, IN18.
            NEW HARMONY HISTORIC DISTRICT, IN159.

                              * * *

PA80   HISTORIC BETHLEHEM, INC.

        516 Main Street
        Bethlehem, PA 18018
        (215) 868-6311

PA80   (Historic Bethlehem, Inc.)
cont.
       Karen Zerbe Huetter, Curator
       Staff: 15 permanent, 30 volunteer

       Restored and reconstructed buildings housing collec-
       tions relating to Moravian settlement of Bethlehem
       (1741); buildings include Gristmiller's House (1782),
       J. S. Goundie House (1810), reconstructed springhouse
       (1764), tannery (1761), waterworks (1762), flour mill
       (1869). Collections include furniture, lighting
       devices, clothing, agricultural tools, food processing
       and service articles, leatherworking tools, waterworks,
       textileworking tools, woodworking tools, other tools,
       decorative arts, games, toys, blueprints; historical
       photographs (see below).

       Dates: 1741-1850.

       100% cataloged; 95% photographed; library and archive.

       Hours: Office, M-F 9-5; 18th-century Industrial Area
       T-Sat 10-4. Appointment recommended. Anyone may use
       collections. Admission fee charged. No fee to use
       library.

       Lends items under certain circumstances. Ca. 7,000
       photographs (4,000 b&w and color prints, 3,000 b&w and
       color slides) relating to Bethlehem and Moravian
       history and Historic Bethlehem's programs and collec-
       tions. Available (on appointment) for research and
       for duplication for a fee.

       Cf. ANNIE S. KEMERER MUSEUM, PA81.
           ARCHIVES OF THE MORAVIAN CHURCH, NORTHERN PROVINCE,
             PA82.
           MORAVIAN MUSEUMS OF BETHLEHEM, PA83.
           BETHLEHEM HISTORIC DISTRICT I, SUBDISTRICT A, PA212.
           GRISTMILLER'S HOUSE, PA213.
           MORAVIAN SUN INN, PA214.
           OLD WATERWORKS, PA215.

                            * * *

PA81   ANNIE S. KEMERER MUSEUM

       427 North New Street
       Bethlehem, PA   18018
       (215) 868-6868

       Mrs. Byron C. Hayes, Director
       Staff: 3 permanent, 50 volunteer

       Restored home of Annie S. Kemerer houses bedding,
       furniture, agricultural tools, firefighting equipment,
       food processing and service articles, clocks, woodwork-
       ing tools, fractur. Many Moravian articles.

       Dates: mostly 19th century.

       75% cataloged; library.

                                              Pennsylvania

PA81   (Annie S. Kemerer Museum)
cont.
        Hours: M-Sat 1-4, 2nd & 4th Sun 2-4. Appointment
        necessary for research. Collections available to all.
        No admission or research fees.

        Occasionally lends materials for study and exhibit.

                              * * *

PA82   ARCHIVES OF THE MORAVIAN CHURCH, NORTHERN PROVINCE

        41 West Locust Street
        Bethlehem, PA 18018
        (215) 866-3255

        Rev. Vernon Nelson, Archivist
        Staff: 2 permanent full-time, 3 part-time

        The Moravians in America were required to gain approval
        from the mother colony in Herrnhut for any new build-
        ings; they sent plans and elevations of all proposed
        new structures to Europe and these were later returned.
        As a result, Moravian architecture is perhaps the best-
        documented of any American group. The Moravian
        Archives in Bethlehem hold the originals and copies of
        the plans of many extant and destroyed Moravian
        buildings in Bethlehem, Salem, and other Moravian
        communities. The Archives' collections also include
        historical photographs of Moravian dwellings; portraits
        and paintings by Moravian artists, notably Haidt;
        fractur, other decorative arts, containers.

        Dates: 1740-1900.

        Library, archives.

        Hours: M-F 9-12, 1-5. Appointment recommended.
        Resources available to bona fide researchers. No
        admission or research fees.

        No loans.

        Cf. MORAVIAN MUSIC FOUNDATION, NC64.
            OLD SALEM, INC., NC65.

                              * * *

PA83   MORAVIAN MUSEUMS OF BETHLEHEM

        66 West Church Street
        Bethlehem, PA 18018
        (215) 867-0173

        Jeanette B. Zug, President
        Staff: 70 volunteer

        Owned by the Moravian Congregation of Bethlehem.

        Several buildings including the Moravian Historical
        Museum (1741), the Apothecary Museum, and the Sun Inn
        (formerly Moravian Inn). Collections include bedding,
        furniture, lighting devices, adornments, clothing,

                                              Pennsylvania

PA83   (Moravian Museums of Bethlehem)
cont.   toilet articles, medical equipment, musical instru-
        ments (including an hydrodaktyopsychicharmonica),
        clocks, woodworking tools, decorative arts, games,
        toys; maps and prints of Bethlehem.

        Dates: as early as 1415; mostly 1742-1875.

        100% cataloged; 50% photographed; library.

        Hours: T-Sat 1-4. Appointment necessary. Resources
        available to anyone during open hours. Admission
        adult $1.00, children 50¢. No fee for use of library.

        Cf. OLD SALEM, INC., NC65.
            MORAVIAN SUN INN, PA214.

                            * * *

PA84   MERCER MUSEUM OF THE BUCKS COUNTY HISTORICAL SOCIETY

        Pine & Ashland Streets
        Doylestown, PA   18901
        (215) 345-0210

        Lynne Poirier, Chief Curator
        Staff: 20 permanent, 200 volunteer

        Immense and varied collection of Pennsylvania German
        materials including bedding, furniture, adornments,
        clothing, toilet articles, agricultural tools, arma-
        ments, food processing and service articles, house-
        keeping tools, musical instruments, textileworking
        tools, woodworking tools, other tools, advertising
        media, fractur, transport, Conestoga wagon, stoveplates,
        games, toys, containers.

        Dates: 18th & 19th centuries.

        10% cataloged; 10% photographed; library.

        Hours: T-Sun 10-5, open Mondays Memorial Day-Labor
        Day, closed Jan & Feb. Appointment necessary for
        special use of museum collections. Collections
        available to public. Admission adult $2.00. Library
        use fee adult $2.00 per day.

        Absolutely no loans.

                            * * *

PA85   NORTHAMPTON COUNTY HISTORICAL & GENEALOGICAL SOCIETY

        101 South Fourth Street
        Easton, PA   18042
        (215) 253-1222

        Mrs. Hilton N. Rahn, Jr., Curator
        (215) 868-1789
        Staff: volunteer

        Society maintains a stone schoolhouse (1778) and
        Mixsell House (1833). Structures house collections

PA85   (Northampton County Historical & Genealogical Society)
cont.
       of bedding, furniture, lighting devices, adornments,
       clothing, agricultural tools, armaments, firefighting
       equipment, food processing and service articles,
       housekeeping tools, musical instruments, textileworking
       tools, woodworking tools, fractur, maps, decorative
       arts, paintings of local scenes and persons, toys.

       Dates: mid-1700's-World War I.

       100% cataloged; little photographed; library.

       Hours vary. Appointment necessary. Resources available
       to public; special collections to serious researchers.
       No admission or research fees.

       Occasionally lends items.

                              * * *

PA86   EPHRATA CLOISTER

       632 West Main Street
       R. D. #1
       Ephrata, PA 17522
       (717) 733-6600

       John L. Kraft, Curator
       Staff: 12 permanent, 1 volunteer

       Governed by the Pennsylvania Historical & Museum
       Commission.

       Restorations of two original buildings of the Ephrata
       Cloister (founded by German Pietist mystic Conrad
       Beissel in 1732), and reconstructions of several others.
       Beissel Cabin (ca. 1748), Hill Cabin (ca. 1750),
       Householder Cabin (ca. 1760), Sisters' House (1743,
       restored), log stables (mid-18th century & recon-
       structed), bakeoven (ca. 1770), two outhouses (recon-
       structed), print shop (1735), weaver's shop (ca. 1750),
       bakehouse (ca. 1748), Saal (1741, restored), Academy
       (1837), Almonry Inn (ca. 1750). Other original and
       reproduced materials include bedding, furniture,
       lighting devices, adornments, clothing, toilet
       articles, agricultural tools, food processing and
       service articles, housekeeping tools, textileworking
       tools, woodworking tools, other tools, bibles, fractur,
       containers.

       Dates: 1750-1850.

       100% cataloged; 1% photographed; library.

       Hours: M-F 8:30-5, Sat 10-4, Sun 12-5. Appointment
       necessary for research. Resources available to all
       serious researchers. No admission or research fees.

       Lends items for study and exhibit. Black & white
       reproductions of letters from the ABC Book of Letter

                                          Pennsylvania

PA86   (Ephrata Cloister)
cont.
       Styles for Fraktur-Schriften (1750) available for
       purchase.

       National Register Site.
       National Historic Landmark.
       Historic American Buildings Survey.

                            * * *

PA87   WILLIAM PENN MEMORIAL MUSEUM AND ARCHIVES

       Third & North Streets
       P. O. Box 1026
       Harrisburg, PA   17108
       (717) 787-4980

       Bruce Bazelon, Registrar
       Staff: 125 permanent

       Affiliated with the Pennsylvania Historical & Museum
       Commission.

       Collection includes bedding, furniture, lighting
       devices, adornments, clothing, toilet articles, agri-
       cultural tools, food processing and service articles,
       housekeeping tools, musical instruments, textileworking
       tools, woodworking tools, other tools, transport
       (including Conestoga wagons), fractur, decorative arts,
       games, toys, containers.

       Dates: 1700-1930.

       100% cataloged; 10% photographed; library.

       Hours: M-Sat 9-5, Sun 1-5. Appointment necessary.
       Resources may be available upon application. No
       admission or research fees.

       Lends items for research and exhibit.

                            * * *

PA88   HERSHEY MUSEUM OF AMERICAN LIFE

       One Chocolate Avenue
       Hershey, PA   17033
       (717) 274-2273

       John W. Strawbridge, Director
       Staff: 6 permanent, 10 volunteer

       Operated by Hershey Estates.

       About one-half of collection is German-American
       including bedding, furniture, lighting devices, adorn-
       ments, clothing, agricultural tools, food processing
       and service tools, housekeeping tools, musical instru-
       ments, textileworking tools, woodworking tools, other
       tools, fractur, land transport, decorative arts, toys;
       George Danner Collection. New Pennsylvania German
       exhibits scheduled for 1979.

                                          Pennsylvania

PA88   (Hershey Museum of American Life)
cont.   Dates: 1760-1900.

Cataloging & photographing in progress; eventually
100% of collection will be cataloged and photographed;
no library.

Hours: Mid-May--Labor Day, daily 9-5; Sep--mid-May
T-Sun 10-5. Appointment necessary. Resources
available to any qualified person with scholarly
interest. $1.25 adult admission.

Lends items for special exhibits.

                            * * *

PA89   AMISH FARM AND HOUSE, INC.

2395 Lincoln Highway East
Lancaster, PA 17602
(717) 394-6185

A. Neuber, Owner
Staff: 14-20 permanent, summers only

Reconstruction/restoration of Old Order Amish farmstead including stone house (1805), stone barn (1803),
well, limekiln, limestone quarry (1802), and many
reconstructed outbuildings. Collections include
originals and reproductions of bedding, furniture,
lighting devices, clothing, toilet articles, food
processing and service articles, housekeeping tools,
textileworking tools, clocks, woodworking tools, other
tools, fractur, land transport (including Conestoga
wagon), decorative arts, games, toys, containers.

Dates: 1802-present.

0% cataloged; 50% photographed; library.

Hours: Winter daily 8:30-4; spring & fall daily
8:30-5; summer daily 8:30-8. Appointment necessary
for research. All researchers welcome. Admission fee
for museum, none for library.

Materials lent for study and exhibit.

                            * * *

PA90   HANS HERR HOUSE

1849 Hans Herr Drive
Lancaster, PA 17602
(717) 464-4438

Staff: 1 permanent, 12 volunteer

Affiliated with the Lancaster Mennonite Conference
Historical Society.

Oldest house in Lancaster County (1719), and oldest
Mennonite meeting place in the United States. Society

PA90   (Hans Herr House)
cont.
        also maintains other restored outbuildings on grounds,
        including barn. Collections include bedding, furni-
        ture, lighting devices, agricultural tools, food pro-
        cessing and service articles, housekeeping tools,
        textileworking tools, woodworking tools, transport.

        Dates: 18th-19th centuries.

        99% cataloged; 0% photographed; no library.

        House: May-Oct 9-4 daily, Nov-Apr 10-3 daily; closed
        Sunday, Christmas, New Year's, Thanksgiving. No
        appointment necessary. Resources available to public.
        Small admission fee charged.

        No loans.

        National Register Site.
        Historic American Buildings Survey.

                              * * *

PA91   LANCASTER COUNTY HISTORICAL SOCIETY

        230 North President Avenue
        Lancaster, PA 17603
        (717) 392-4633

        John Ward Willson Loose, President
        Staff: 4 permanent, 9 volunteer

        Society concentrates on research and publication;
        most holdings are books, manuscripts, documents.
        Small museum collection includes clothing, food
        processing and service articles, fractur, decorative
        arts, toys.

        Dates: 1710-present.

        Library.

        Hours: T-Sat 9:30-4:30, Th 9:30-9. Anyone may use
        research facilities for a fee. Members free; non-
        members must become Research Fellows ($5.00 per year)
        or College Student Research Fellows ($2.00 per year)
        or obtain special One Day Pass ($1.00).

        Lends items under certain conditions. Black & white
        and color prints exist of Lancaster County structures
        and of land transport.

                              * * *

PA92   LANCASTER MENNONITE CONFERENCE HISTORICAL SOCIETY

        2215 Mill Stream Road
        Lancaster, PA 17602
        (717) 393-9745

        Carolyn L. Charles, Director
        Staff: 5 permanent full-time, 3 part-time, 3-50
                volunteer

                                              Pennsylvania

PA92   (Lancaster Mennonite Conference Historical Society)
cont. Small collection of bedding, furniture, lighting
       devices, clothing, agricultural tools, food processing
       and service articles, housekeeping tools, other tools,
       fractur, decorative arts, toys, containers.

Dates: 1525-present.

25% cataloged; 30% photographed; library.

Hours: T-Sat 8:30-5, M 8:30-9. No appointment
necessary. Resources available to all. No admission
or research fees.

Rarely lends items.

* * *

PA93   PENNSYLVANIA FARM MUSEUM OF LANDIS VALLEY

2451 Kissel Hill Road
Lancaster, PA 17601
(717) 569-0401

Carroll J. Hopf, Director
Staff: 33 permanent, 15 volunteer

Affiliated with the Pennsylvania Historical & Museum
Commission.

One-hundred-acre tract depicting Pennsylvania country
life ca. 1750-1900. Included are over 20 buildings
and extensive collections, about 40% of which relate
to local Pennsylvania Germans. German buildings:
Landis House (1870), Seamstress House (1790), Settler's
Farm (1760), Federal Farmstead (early 19th century),
Print Shop/Harness Shop (1800), Blacksmith Shop (late
19th century), Tin Shop (19th century), Maple Grove
School (1890), Landis Valley House (hotel, 1856).
Collections include bedding, furniture, lighting
devices, clothing, agricultural tools, armaments, food
processing and service articles, housekeeping tools,
metalworking tools, musical instruments, textileworking
tools, woodworking tools, other tools, transport
(including a Conestoga wagon), fractur, advertising
media, maps, decorative arts, games, toys, containers.

Dates: 1780-1920.

25% cataloged; 5% photographed; library.

Hours: M-Sat, holidays 8:30-5, Sun 12-4:30. Appointment necessary for research. Resources available to
students, collectors, anyone else doing serious
research. No admission or library use charges for
researchers. General admission adult $1.00, over 65
and under 12 free.

Occasionally lends items. Black & white prints exist
for many items. Slides exist for structures, fractur.

* * *

PA94 PENNSYLVANIA DUTCH FOLK CULTURE SOCIETY, INC.

Lenhartsville, PA   19534
(215) 562-4803

Florence Baver, Director & Curator
Staff: 2 permanent, volunteers as needed

Society maintains two small restored houses and
restored school in addition to Folklife Museum and barn
housing collection of horse-drawn farm machinery.
Other collections include clothing and decorative arts.

Dates: 18th century-early 20th century.

50% cataloged; 10% photographed; small library.

Hours: June-Aug Sat&Sun 10-5; Apr-June, Sep-Nov
Sat&Sun 1-5. No appointment necessary during regular
hours. Resources available to public. Admission and
library use fees.

No loans.

* * *

PA95 UNION COUNTY HISTORICAL SOCIETY MUSEUM

Union County Courthouse
Lewisburg, PA   17837
(717) 524-4461 ext. 56

Jeannette Lasansky
Staff: 3 volunteer

No organized museum collection. Oral Tradition/Folk
Culture Program is developing an extensive collection
of tapes, many concerning material culture, e.g. food
processing, basketry, broommaking, blacksmithing, tin-
smithing, cabinetry, barn raising, farming, flour
mills, ice houses, Mooresburg pottery, school, Pennsylvania (Kentucky) rifles, quilting, weaving. Slides
and photographs in the collection correspond to tape
topics; plus portraits.

Dates: collected in 1970's.

100% cataloged; oral history library.

Hours: By appointment only. Anyone may use collections for research. No research fees.

Lends tapes, slides, and transcripts.

* * *

PA96 THE MORAVIAN CONGREGATION, LITITZ

Church Square
Lititz, PA   17543
(717) 626-8515

Wayne B. LeFevre, President, Archives Committee
Mrs. Richard Allebach, Tour Director
Staff: 18 Museum Committee members
        15 tour guides   Pennsylvania

PA96   (The Moravian Congregation, Lititz)
cont.
         Congregation maintains five structures including the
         only extant Moravian Corpse House (or Dead House) in
         America (1786)--the dead were kept here before burial;
         also Gemeinhaus (1763) with restored lovefeast kitchen;
         Lititz Moravian Church (1787), oldest Moravian church
         in continuous use in America; Single Brothers' House
         (1759). Collections include Moravian furniture
         (including long-legged trombone chairs and a Windsor
         organ bench), lighting devices, adornments, clothing,
         agricultural tools, food processing and service
         articles, housekeeping tools, musical instruments
         (including two Tannenberg organs), textileworking
         tools, firefighting apparatus, fractur, decorative
         arts, containers.

         Dates: 1760-1920.

         75-80% cataloged; 98% photographed; library.

         Hours: By appointment only. Resources available to
         qualified scholars and researchers. Admission fee
         $1.00. No established fee for use of library.

         Occasionally lends items. Prints and slides exist
         for many articles.

                                 * * *

PA97   MUSEUM OF THE MORAVIAN HISTORICAL SOCIETY

         214 East Center Street
         Route 191
         Nazareth, PA 18064
         (215) 759-0291

         Mr. Eschor Clewell, Curator
         Staff: 1 permanent

         George Whitefield House (1740-43) houses Moravian
         furniture, lighting devices, clothing, agricultural
         tools, musical instruments, textileworking tools,
         woodworking tools, fractur, decorative arts, stove-
         plates, games, toys, containers.

         Dates: 1740-1850.

         0% cataloged; 0% photographed; small library.

         Hours: TFSat & 2nd & 4th Sun 2-5. Facilities not yet
         ready to accommodate researchers. No admission fee.

         No loans.

                                 * * *

PA98   SCHWENKFELDER LIBRARY & MUSEUM

         One Seminary Avenue
         Pennsburg, PA 18073
         (215) 679-7175

PA98   (Schwenkfelder Library & Museum)
cont.   Claire E. Conway, Administrator
         Staff: 2 permanent

Large collection includes bedding, furniture, lighting
devices, adornments, clothing, toilet articles, agricultural tools, food processing and service articles,
housekeeping tools, musical instruments, textileworking
tools, woodworking tools, other tools, fractur, transport, decorative arts, toys, games, containers;
historical photographs.

Dates: 1730-present.

80% cataloged; 5% photographed; library.

Hours: Daily 9-4. Appointment recommended. Collections open to public. No admission or research charges.

Rarely lends articles.

                          * * *

PA99   FREE LIBRARY OF PHILADELPHIA

         Logan Square
         Philadelphia, PA   19103
         (215) 686-5405

●Print and Picture Department

Robert F. Looney, Head
Staff: 4 permanent (Department)

Historical photographs and other pictures of 18th-20th
century Philadelphia including buildings, churches,
festivals, street scenes.

Dates: ca. 1700-present.

Collections arranged by subject; library.

Hours: M-Sat 9-5. Appointment recommended. Resources
open to public. No admission or research fees.

Some material may be borrowed for three weeks. No
reproduction rights fees.

                          - - -

●Rare Book Department

(215) 686-5416

Howell J. Heaney, Rare Book Librarian
Staff: 6 permanent (Department)

Over 100 examples of fractur and over 2000 Pennsylvania
German broadsides. Published catalog of fractur
collection.

Dates: 1745-1850.

90% cataloged; 90% photographed; library.

                                        Pennsylvania

PA99   (Free Library of Philadelphia--Rare Book Department)
cont.
        Hours: M-Sat 9-5. No appointment necessary.
        Collection open to serious researchers. No admission
        or research charges.

        Lends materials for special exhibitions only.

                              * * *

PA100 GERMAN SOCIETY OF PENNSYLVANIA
       Joseph M. Horner Memorial Library

       611 Spring Garden Street
       Philadelphia, PA   19123
       (215) 627-4365

       Mrs. Pohl
       Mrs. Richardson
       Staff: 2½ permanent

       Fractur, bibles, decorative arts including bronze
       models of statues by J. Otto Schweizer. Historical
       photographs and ephemera of Philadelphia German
       community, local German-American societies, etc.

       Dates: end of 18th century-present.

       90% cataloged; library.

       Hours: W 10-5, Th 10-6, Sat 10-4. Appointment
       recommended. Open to members, researchers, anyone
       who contacts Society with specific problems regarding
       German-language materials.

       No admission or research fees. Borrowing fees charged.

       Occasionally lends materials.

                              * * *

PA101 GERMANTOWN HISTORICAL SOCIETY

       5214 Germantown Avenue
       Philadelphia, PA   19144
       (215) 844-0514

       Leonard Rossiter Denis, Assistant Secretary & Librarian
       Staff: 5 permanent, 15 volunteer

       Germantown was first German settlement in North America.
       Society maintains seven buildings: Baynton House
       (ca. 1800), library; Conyngham-Hacker House (ca. 1772),
       furniture, clocks, china, silver; Von Trott Museum,
       kitchen, farm, industrial implements, firebacks,
       sleds, sleighs; Howell House (ca. 1770), bedding, toys;
       Clarkson-Watson House (ca. 1740), clothing; Wyck House
       (ca. 1690), oldest house in Germantown; Ebenezer
       Maxwell House (ca. 1860), Victorian museum and study
       center; Deshler-Morris House (ca. 1772), the "German-
       town White House." Total holdings include bedding

                                              Pennsylvania

PA101   (Germantown Historical Society)
cont.   (including 200 quilts), furniture, lighting devices,
         500 pieces of clothing, toilet articles, agricultural
         tools, food processing and service articles, housekeep-
         ing tools, musical instruments, textileworking tools,
         woodworking tools, Conestoga wagon, fractur, decorative
         arts, games, toys, containers.

         Dates: 1683-present.

         85-90% cataloged; 2% photographed; library (Baynton
         House).

         Hours: TWTh 1-5 and by appointment. Appointment
         necessary for group tours and research projects.
         Resources available to members and anyone with a
         serious interest. Admission fee adult $1.00, children
         50¢. No fee for use of library.

         Black & white prints of many items exist. Color
         slides and prints exist for some furniture and the
         Conestoga wagon.

         Cf. BEGGARSTOWN SCHOOL, PA227.
            COLONIAL GERMANTOWN HISTORIC DISTRICT, PA228.
            MENNONITE MEETINGHOUSE, PA229.

                              * * *

PA102   HISTORICAL SOCIETY OF PENNSYLVANIA

         13th & Locust Streets
         Philadelphia, PA   19107
         (215) 732-6200

         Peter J. Parker, Curator of Manuscripts
         Staff: 22 permanent, 3 volunteer

         Bibliographic and pictorial material and a few
         artifacts relating to history of Pennsylvania, in
         particular the city of Philadelphia. Ephemera relating
         to German population can be found in "Society Collec-
         tion," Box 7A: "Redemptioners and Palatines in
         Philadelphia 1768-1803," Box 6A: "Germantown Items,"
         ledgers and records of Manheim Glass Factory, materials
         from German Settlement Society, Rittenhouse business
         documents, Declaration of Independence in German
         (printed July 9, 1776). Also furniture, maps, lighting
         devices, musical instruments, textileworking tools,
         fractur, decorative arts, games, toys, containers.
         Also Abraham Cassel Collection of Manuscript Music
         from Ephrata.

         Dates: 1720-1840.

         15% cataloged; 2% photographed; library.

         Hours: M 1-9, T-F 9-5; closed national holidays.
         Appointment necessary for museum objects. Library

PA102 (Historical Society of Pennsylvania)
cont.
       open to all; manuscripts and objects in storage
       available upon application. No fee to members, other-
       wise $1.00 per day, $7.50 for six weeks.

       Lends items for study and exhibit. A few prints and
       slides exist for German-American materials in the
       collections.

                              * * *

PA103 PHILADELPHIA MUSEUM OF ART

       Benjamin Franklin Parkway at 26th Street
       P. O. Box 7646
       Philadelphia, PA 19101
       (215) 763-8100

       ●American Art Department

       Beatrice B. Garvan, Associate Curator of American Art
       Staff: 3 permanent, interns (Department)

       Very large collection of Pennsylvania German and
       other German-American materials including bedding,
       furniture, armaments, food processing and service
       articles, clocks, decorative arts (including many
       samplers), stoveplates, fractur.

       Dates: 1700-1900.

       100% cataloged; 100% photographed; library.

       Hours: Daily 9-5. Appointment recommended for
       research. Resources available to students and museum
       members. No admission fee. Library use fee for non-
       members.

       Lends items for exhibit. Illustrated handbook to
       museum collections is being developed.

                              - - -

       ●Rights and Reproductions Department

       Lois Glewwe, Department Head
       Staff: 3 permanent (Department)

       Slide Library for staff use only. Business by mail
       only.

       Slides of ca. 200 of the German-American items in the
       American Art Department (described above) and other
       institutions available for purchase at 85¢-$1.25 per
       slide depending on quantity ordered. Catalog informa-
       tion sent free of charge with rate sheets and order
       forms. Pre-paid orders taken through mail.

       Dates: 1700-1850.

                              * * *

Pennsylvania

PA104 HISTORICAL SOCIETY OF SCHUYLKILL COUNTY

> 14 North Third Street
> Pottsville, PA   17901
> (717) 622-7540

> Reginald Rix, Curator
> Staff: 1 permanent, 2 volunteer

> Small museum collection includes bedding, furniture,
> lighting devices, food processing and service articles,
> housekeeping tools, musical instruments, textileworking
> tools, woodworking tools, other tools, fractur; over
> 5000 historical photographs; over 1200 slides of
> Schuylkill County scenes.

> Dates: 1875-1945.

> 100% cataloged; 0% photographed; library.

> Hours: T-Sat 10-12, 1-4; Th 1-9. No appointment
> necessary. Resources available to all. No admission
> or research fees.

> No loans.

* * *

PA105 HISTORICAL SOCIETY OF BERKS COUNTY

> 940 Center Avenue
> Reading, PA   19601
> (215) 375-4375

> Harold E. Yoder, Jr., Executive Director
> Staff: 4 permanent full-time, 6 part-time

> Large collection relating to history of German settlers
> in Berks County, PA, including bedding, furniture,
> lighting devices, adornments, clothing, agricultural
> tools, food processing and service articles, house-
> keeping tools, musical instruments, woodworking tools,
> other tools, fractur, transport (including Conestoga
> wagon), decorative arts, toys; historical photographs.

> Dates: 18th century-present.

> 100% cataloged; 10% photographed; library.

> Hours: T-Sat 9-4. Appointment necessary for archival
> material only. Open to public. Admission fees:
> free to members, 50¢ non-members for museum, $1.00
> per day non-members for library.

> Lends items for study and exhibition.

* * *

PA106 READING PUBLIC MUSEUM & ART GALLERY

> 500 Museum Road
> Reading, PA   19611
> (215) 373-1525

PA106 (Reading Public Museum & Art Gallery)
cont. J. Daniel Selig, Director
       Staff: 25 permanent, volunteer tour guides

       Large collection includes bedding, furniture, lighting
       devices, adornments, clothing, agricultural tools,
       food processing and service articles, housekeeping
       tools, textileworking tools, woodworking tools, fractur,
       decorative arts, games, toys, containers.

       Dates: 1700-1900.

       100% cataloged; 100% photographed by end of 1979;
       library.

       Hours: M-F 9-5, Sat 9-12, Sun 2-5. Appointment/
       permission from Director's office necessary to use
       collections for research. Resources available to
       anyone. No admission or research fees.

       Lends items to other institutions and museums.

                              * * *

PA107 THOMAS R. BRENDLE MEMORIAL LIBRARY & MUSEUM

       Schaefferstown, PA 17088
       no phone

       John Hickernell
       Staff: volunteer, varies

       Administered by Historic Schaefferstown, Inc.

       Collection of documents, manuscripts, bibles, tools,
       and furnishings relating to German-Swiss settlers of
       area; oral history project; tapes of John Brendle's
       Pennsylvania-German dialect broadcasts.

       Dates: early 18th century-1900.

       Library.

       Hours: Sat&Sun 1-5, weekdays by appointment.
       Resources available to public.

       Cf. ALEXANDER SCHAEFFER FARM MUSEUM, PA108.
           BRENDLE FARMS, PA230.

                              * * *

PA108 ALEXANDER SCHAEFFER FARM MUSEUM

       Schaefferstown, PA 17088
       no phone

       John Hickernell
       Staff: volunteer, varies

       Living historical farm. Farmstead includes restored
       Swiss Bank House (1737), Swiss Bank Barn, cider

PA108 (Alexander Schaeffer Farm Museum)
cont. mill; agricultural tools, food processing and service
       articles, land transport.

Dates: early 18th century-1900.

Library.

Hours: June 15-Labor Day M-F 10-4, Sat&Sun 12-4.
No appointment necessary to visit farm. Resources not
yet ready to accommodate researchers. Admission fees
adult $1.00, children 25¢. Special group rates.

Cf. THOMAS R. BRENDLE MEMORIAL LIBRARY & MUSEUM, PA107.
    BRENDLE FARMS, PA230.

                          * * *

PA109 BROWN BROTHERS STOCK PHOTOS

P. O. Box 50
Sterling, PA 18463
(717) 689-9688

Harry B. Collins, Jr., President
Staff: 2 permanent

Large (ca. 6 million items) commercial collection of
pictures on all topics. Of the four large commercial
repositories described here (Bettman, Black Star,
Culver, Brown Brothers), Brown Brothers is the best
for historical, immigration, and ethnic materials.

Dates: pre-history-present.

Mail and phone orders from qualified researchers.

Material lent. Reproduction rights fees charged.

                          * * *

PA110 MONROE COUNTY HISTORICAL SOCIETY

Ninth & Main Streets
Stroudsburg, PA 18360
no phone

Mrs. Horace G. Walters, Curator
Staff: 1 permanent, 5 volunteer

Affiliated with East Stroudsburg State College.

Collections include bedding, furniture, lighting
devices, food processing and service articles, housekeeping tools, textileworking tools, woodworking tools,
fractur, containers.

Dates: 19th century.

Very little cataloged or photographed; library.

Hours: T 1-4; appointment necessary other times.
Resources available to general public. No admission or
research fees.

No loans.

                          * * *   Pennsylvania

PA111 QUIET VALLEY LIVING HISTORICAL FARM

R. D. #2
P. O. Box 2495
Stroudsburg, PA 18360
(717) 992-6161

Sue W. Oiler, Manager
Staff: 3 permanent full-time, 15 part-time,
        25 volunteer

Administered by Historical Farm Association, Inc.

Farmstead consists of restored Bank House (1765),
restored Bank Barn (1850), two tool sheds (1920),
corncrib, restored springhouse (1765), and reconstructed
bakeoven, smokehouse, icehouse, dryhouse. Each building
contains appropriate collection illustrative of region's
rural life during 19th century.

Dates: 1765-1892.

0% cataloged; 0% photographed; small library.

Hours: May 1-June 19--groups by appointment; June 20-
Labor Day M-Sat 9:30-5:30, Sun 1-5:30. Research
facilities available to staff only. Admission fee
charged. No library use fee.

Does not lend items at present.

National Register Site.

                          * * *

PA112 CONRAD WEISER HOMESTEAD

R. D. #1
P. O. Box 1028
Womelsdorf, PA 19567
(215) 589-2934

J. Paul Hertzog, Custodial Guide
Staff: 2 permanent

Governed by the Pennsylvania Historical & Museum
Commission.

Home of Conrad Weiser, German immigrant who played an
important role in the relations between the Indians
and the colonists in Pennsylvania. Site includes
limestone house (1729) and log cabin (1800). Small
collection includes furniture, food processing and
service articles, housekeeping tools.

Dates: 1729-1800.

100% cataloged; 100% photographed; library.

Hours: T-Sat 10-5, Sun-M 1-5. No appointment
necessary. Anyone may use collections and library for
research. Admission fee 50¢. Library use fee 50¢.
Students and senior citizens free.

PA112 (Conrad Weiser Homestead)
cont. No loans.

       National Register Site.
       National Historic Landmark.

                            * * *

PA113 PETER WENTZ FARMSTEAD

       Route 73 (Schultz Road)
       Worcester, PA 19490
       (215) 584-5104

       Albert T. Gamon, Director/Administrator
       Staff: 5 permanent, 70 volunteer

       Restored 1777 house showing both German and Welsh
       influences. German material in collection includes
       bedding, furniture, lighting devices, clothing, agri-
       cultural tools, textileworking tools, woodworking
       tools, other tools, transport, decorative arts, stove-
       plates, toys, containers.

       Dates: 18th century.

       100% cataloged; 50% photographed; small library.

       Hours: T-Sat 10-4, Sun 1-4. No appointment necessary.
       Anyone may use research facilities. No admission or
       research fees.

       No loans. Black & white prints and color slides exist
       for many objects.

       National Register Site.

                            * * *

PA114 THE HISTORICAL SOCIETY OF YORK COUNTY

       250 East Market Street
       York, PA 17403
       (717) 848-1587

       Douglas C. Dolan, Executive Director
       Staff: 12 permanent, 50 volunteer

       Society maintains four restorations, three of German
       origin: Golden Plough Tavern (1741), General Gates
       House (1751), Bobb Log House (1812). Large collection
       of German-Americana includes bedding, furniture,
       lighting devices, adornments, clothing, toilet articles,
       agricultural tools, food processing and service
       articles, housekeeping tools, musical instruments
       (including 1804 Tannenberg Organ), textileworking
       tools, other tools, transport, fractur, decorative
       arts, toys, games, containers, Conestoga wagon; Lewis
       Miller Collection; historical photographs.

       Dates: 1721-present.

                                       Pennsylvania

PA114 (The Historical Society of York County)
cont. 95% cataloged; museum 1% photographed; library.

Hours: Museum M-Sat 9-5, Sun 1-5; Restorations M-Sat
10-4, Sun 1-4:30. Library MWFSat 9-5, TTh 1-5.
Appointment necessary for research. Resources
available to public. Admission fees for museum
adult $1.00, children 50¢; library free for members,
non-members $1.00 per day.

Lends items for study and exhibit.

* * *

SD115 HERITAGE HALL MUSEUM AND HISTORICAL LIBRARY

Freeman Junior College
Freeman, SD 57029
(605) 925-4231

Dr. Ralph C. Kauffman, Curator
Staff: 2 permanent, volunteers as needed

Collections include bedding, furniture, lighting
devices, clothing, adornments, toilet articles, agricultural tools, food processing and service articles,
housekeeping tools, musical instruments, textileworking
tools, woodworking tools, other tools, transport,
decorative arts, games, toys, containers. Nineteenth-
century church and schoolhouse remain to be developed.

Dates: 1874-1950.

100% cataloged; 2-4% photographed; library.

Hours: By appointment. Generally no restrictions on
research. No admission or research fees.

Occasionally lends materials.

* * *

SD116 SOUTH DAKOTA STATE HISTORICAL SOCIETY
South Dakota Historical Resource Center

Memorial Building
Pierre, SD 57501
(605) 224-3615

Bonnie Gardner
Staff: 7 permanent (Resource Center)

Historical photographs of Hutterite colonies in South
Dakota including 17 of Bon Homme Hutterite Colony;
Germans from Russia in Eureka and Pukwana, South
Dakota.

Dates: late 19th century.

Library.

Hours: M-F 8-12, 1-5. No appointment necessary.
Resources available to public. No admission or
research charges.

No loans.   Pennsylvania-South Dakota
                        * * *

SD117 W. H. OVER MUSEUM

> University of South Dakota
> Vermillion, SD   57069
> (605) 677-5228
>
> June Sampson, Director
> Staff: 5 permanent, 25 volunteer
>
> Small number of German-American items including agri-
> cultural tools, housekeeping tools, woodworking tools;
> historical photographs.
>
> Dates: 1880-1920.
>
> 50% cataloged; 0% photographed; library, non-
> circulating.
>
> Hours: M-F 1-4:30, Sat 10-4:30, Sun 2-4:30. No
> appointment necessary for research. Resources
> available to public. No admission or research fees.
>
> Lends items for study and exhibit.

* * *

SD118 SHRINE TO MUSIC MUSEUM

> U. S. D. Box 194
> Vermillion, SD   57069
> (605) 677-5306
>
> Dr. André P. Larson, Director
> Staff: 4 permanent
>
> Affiliated with the University of South Dakota.
>
> Approximately 5-10% of collection pertains to German-
> Americana; Arne B. Larson Collection of Musical
> Instruments & Library; music and musical instruments.
>
> Dates: 1600-present.
>
> 100% cataloged (instruments); library.
>
> Hours: M-F 9-4:30, Sat 10-4:30, Sun 2-4:30. Appoint-
> ment necessary for research. Facilities available to
> qualified scholars and students. Regulations for
> access to collections and research fees available upon
> request.
>
> Lends articles for special exhibits.

* * *

TX119 COMFORT MUSEUM

> Comfort, TX   78013
> (512) 392-5007
>
> Glen E. Lich
> Staff: 2-6 volunteer
>
> Collections include bedding, furniture, lighting
> devices, clothing, adornments, toilet articles, agri-

TX119   (Comfort Museum)
cont.   cultural tools, food processing and service articles,
        housekeeping tools, musical instruments, textileworking
        tools, other tools, fractur, transport, decorative
        arts, games, toys, containers; portraits.

        0% cataloged; 10% photographed; no library.

        Hours: By appointment only. Resources available to
        any serious researcher or archivist. No admission
        fee.

        Rarely lends items for study or research. Black &
        white prints exist of area structures.

                              * * *

TX120   ADMIRAL NIMITZ CENTER

        340 East Main Street
        P. O. Box 777
        Fredericksburg, TX   78624
        (512) 997-4379

        Douglass Hubbard, Executive Director
        Cheryl Demuth, Accessionist
        Staff: 7 permanent, 1 volunteer

        Affiliated with the Fleet Admiral Chester W. Nimitz
        Memorial Naval Museum Commission.

        Chiefly a museum celebrating Admiral Chester Nimitz,
        Commander-in-Chief in the Pacific in World War II and
        a native of Fredericksburg (settled in 1846 by Germans).
        Some German materials relate to the Nimitz family and
        early Fredericksburg: furniture, clothing, agricul-
        tural tools, food processing and service articles,
        woodworking tools.

        Dates: 1850-1900.

        100% cataloged; small percentage photographed; library.

        Hours: 8-5 daily. Appointment necessary for research.
        Anyone may use collections for research. Admission
        fee adult $1.00; groups, children, and uniformed
        military personnel free. No charges for use of library.

        Lends items for study and exhibit.

                              * * *

TX121   PIONEER MEMORIAL MUSEUM

        311 West Main Street
        P. O. Box 765
        Fredericksburg, TX   78624
        (512) 997-2835

        Glen Treibs, President
        Staff: 2 permanent, 15-20 volunteer

TX121 (Pioneer Memorial Museum)
cont. Administered by the Gillespie County Historical Society.

Historical Society maintains several buildings:
Vereinskirche (1846, reconstruction): Kammlah House
and Store (1856, now Pioneer Memorial Museum); Fassel
House (1890); Schandau House (1890's); Sunday House
(early 1900's, small house used by farming families
when they came to town/church on weekends; typical of
Germans in Central Texas); smokehouse, hack shed;
First Methodist Church (1856). Collections in Pioneer
Memorial Museum include bedding, furniture, lighting
devices, adornments, clothing, agricultural tools,
housekeeping tools, textileworking tools, woodworking
tools, other tools, decorative arts, toys, containers.

Dates: 1846-1900.

100% cataloged; few photographed; no library.

Hours: Winter Sat 10-5, Sun 1-5; summer M-Sat 10-5,
Sun 1-5. Appointment necessary. Resources available
to anyone. Admission charged for Pioneer Memorial
Museum. No library use fee.

Rarely lends items. A slide show, "The Easter Fires
of Fredericksburg," is available for purchase from the
Institute of Texan Cultures (TX127).

Cf. FREDERICKSBURG HISTORIC DISTRICT, TX237.

                          * * *

TX122 LLANO COUNTY HISTORICAL MUSEUM

223 Ford Street
Llano, TX 78643
(512) 247-4051

Zella Alexander, Director
Staff: 1 permanent

Affiliated with the Llano County Historical Society.

Collections include bedding, furniture, adornments,
clothing, agricultural tools, food processing and
service articles, toys, containers. Also a large
school bell and a vessel for making salt.

Dates: 1850-present.

0% cataloged; 0% photographed; no library.

Hours: June-Aug T-Sun 10-12, 1-5; Sep-May FSatSun 1-5.
No appointment necessary. Resources available to
public. No admission or research fees.

No loans.

                          * * *

TX123 MASON COUNTY MUSEUM

P. O. Box 303
Mason, TX 76856
no phone

Mrs. Hilton Moneyhon, Director
Staff: 1 permanent, 10 volunteer

Native sandstone building (1887) houses small collection of bedding, clothing, adornments, toilet articles,
agricultural tools, food processing and service
articles, musical instruments, woodworking tools.

Dates: 1858-1920.

100% cataloged; 0% photographed; no library.

Hours: June-Sep daily 1-5 and by appointment. No
admission or research fees.

No loans.

Cf. MASON HISTORIC DISTRICT, TX238.

* * *

TX124 SOPHIENBURG MEMORIAL MUSEUM

401 West Coll Street
P. O. Box 398
New Braunfels, TX 78130
(512) 629-1572

Valeska Startz, Director
Staff: 3 permanent, over 150 volunteer

New Braunfels was settled in the 1830's by Germans.
German is still widely spoken here. Sophienburg
collection includes bedding, furniture, lighting
devices, adornments, clothing, toilet articles, agricultural tools, food processing and service articles,
housekeeping tools, musical instruments, textileworking
tools, woodworking tools, fractur, transport, decorative
arts, games, toys, containers; historical photographs.

Dates: 1830-present.

80% cataloged; 10% photographed; library.

Hours: M-F 10-5, Sun 1-5. Appointment necessary for
research. Admission and research fees charged.

No loans of materials at present.

* * *

TX125 WINEDALE HISTORICAL CENTER

P. O. Box 11
Round Top, TX 78954
(713) 278-3530

TX125 (Winedale Historical Center)
cont.
Wayne Bell, Director
Gloria Jaster, Administrator
Staff: 18 permanent

Affiliated with the University of Texas at Austin.

Outdoor museum of cultural history and center for the study of ethnic cultures of Central Texas. Buildings with some German background: Lewis House (1834, 1848), Lone Oak Cottage (1855), McGregor-Grimm House (1861), hay barn (1894). Collections also include bedding, furniture, lighting devices, adornments, clothing, toilet articles, agricultural tools, food processing and service articles, housekeeping tools, musical instruments, textileworking tools, woodworking tools, other tools, transport, fractur, decorative arts, games, toys, containers; historical photographs.

Dates: ca. 1850-1870.

100% cataloged; 25% photographed; small library.

Hours: Sat 9-5, Sun 12-5, T-F by appointment. Appointment necessary for research. Anyone may use resources. Admission fee adults $2.00, students 50¢. No research fees.

Occasionally lends materials to other museums.

* * *

TX126 DAUGHTERS OF THE REPUBLIC OF TEXAS LIBRARY

P. O. Box 2599
San Antonio, TX   78299
(512) 225-1071

Staff: 6 permanent

Photographic archives include three collections on German-American topics: the Eickenroht Collection, Grandjean Collection, and Schuchard Collection.

Dates: 1870-1900.

100% cataloged; negatives for 100% Grandjean Collection; negatives for 50% Eickenroht and Schuchard Collections; library.

Hours: M-F 9-5. No appointment necessary. Collections open to public. No admission or research fees.

No loans.

* * *

TX127 INSTITUTE OF TEXAN CULTURES

Durango Blvd. at I-37
San Antonio, TX   78294
(512) 226-7651

TX127 (Institute of Texan Cultures)
cont.   Laura Bullion, Librarian
        Staff: 100 permanent, 75 volunteer

        Over 5000 historical photographs (from various Texas
        collections) of the lives and history of Texas Germans:
        New Braunfels, Fredericksburg, Galveston, San Antonio;
        organizations, schools, buildings, churches, festivals,
        agricultural scenes. A very fine collection. Also
        museum items on loan from other institutions only.

        Dates: ca. 1800-present.

        Photographs arranged in vertical file; library.

        Hours: Exhibits only T-Sat 9-5, business offices
        (including photographic collection) M-F 8-5. Appoint-
        ment recommended. Anyone may use resources. No
        admission or research fees.

        Loans made usually only to specially produced traveling
        exhibits. Two educational slideshows on Texas Germans
        are available for purchase: "The Cat Spring Germans"
        (72 slides, 1971) and "The Easter Fires of Fredericks-
        burg" (64 slides, 1971). Both make use of historical
        photographs from the Institute's collection.

                              * * *

TX128 VARNER-HOGG PLANTATION STATE PARK

        1702 North 17th Street
        P. O. Box 696
        West Columbia, TX 77486
        (713) 345-4656

        Koren K. Cariker, Curator
        Staff: 10 permanent

        Affiliated with Texas Parks & Wildlife Department.

        Small but fine collection of Texas-German furniture
        and decorative arts; restored kitchen (1835).

        Dates: 19th century.

        Cataloging and photographing in process; no library.

        Hours: TThFSat 10-11:30, 1-4:30; Sun 1-4:30. Appoint-
        ment recommended for research. Collections open to
        public. Admission 50¢ for adults, 25¢ for children
        under 13.

        No loans. Color postcards of furniture available for
        purchase.

                              * * *

VA129 REUEL B. PRITCHETT MUSEUM

        Bridgewater College
        Bridgewater, VA 22812
        (703) 828-2501

                                         Texas-Virginia

VA129 (Reuel B. Pritchett Museum)
cont. J. F. Replogle, Director
       Staff: 1 part-time, 2 volunteer

       Church of the Brethren Collection includes bedding,
       furniture, lighting devices, adornments, clothing,
       toilet articles, agricultural tools, armaments, food
       processing and service articles, housekeeping tools,
       musical instruments, textileworking tools, woodworking
       tools, other tools, fractur, bibles (Sower Bible
       Collection 1743-1776), decorative arts, toys, con-
       tainers.

       Dates: 1743-1978.

       50% cataloged; 0% photographed; library.

       Hours: TTh 1-4, Sun 2-4. Appointment recommended for
       research. Resources available to the public. No
       admission or research fees, but donation requested.

       No loans.

                            * * *

VA130 BLUE RIDGE FARM MUSEUM

       Ferrum, VA 24088
       (703) 365-2121, ext. 107

       Virginia Crook, Curator/Registrar
       Staff: 6 permanent

       Affiliated with Ferrum College.
       Administered by the Blue Ridge Institute.

       Nineteenth-century Virginia-German farmstead restora-
       tion/reconstruction including German log house, three-
       pen German bank barn, kitchen house, dry storage shed,
       with Blue Ridge furniture and artifacts. Scheduled
       date of completion mid-1979. Archives include histori-
       cal photographs of old Virginia-German farms; oral
       history projects and recorded folk music from region.

       Dates: 1770-1900.

       15% cataloged; 0% photographed; archives.

       Hours: M-F 8:30-4:30. Appointment necessary. No
       admission or research fees.

       May lend materials under certain circumstances.

                            * * *

VA131 MENNO SIMONS HISTORICAL LIBRARY & ARCHIVES

       Eastern Mennonite College
       Harrisonburg, VA 22801
       (703) 433-2771

       Grace Showalter, Librarian
       Staff: 1½ permanent

VA131 (Menno Simons Historical Library & Archives)
cont.   Library includes small collection of museum objects
        relating to the history of German settlers in Virginia
        including furniture, clothing, food processing and
        service articles, musical instruments, fractur,
        decorative arts.

        Dates: 1727-present.

        70% cataloged; library.

        Hours: Sep-May M-F 8-12, 1-5; Sat 9-12; summer a.m.
        only; closed during college vacations. Advisable to
        call due to school breaks. Resources available to
        anyone. No admission or research fees.

        Interlibrary loans; occasional loans to exhibits.

                              * * *

VA132 ABBY ALDRICH ROCKEFELLER FOLK ART COLLECTION

        307 South England Street
        Drawer C
        Williamsburg, VA 23185
        (703) 229-1000 ext. 6221

        Rebecca L. Lehman, Registrar
        Staff: 6 permanent, 1-3 volunteer

        Affiliated with the Colonial Williamsburg Foundation.

        Collection of American decorative arts, including
        Pennsylvania German and Moravian materials: fractur,
        toys, containers, decorative arts, portraits.

        Dates: 1790's-1830's, some toys later.

        50% cataloged; 99% photographed; library.

        Hours: Winter daily 12-6, summer daily 10-9.
        Appointment necessary for research. Resources
        available to anyone involved in a legitimate research
        project. No admission or research charges.

        Lends articles for exhibit and for study under special
        circumstances. 8" x 10" b&w glossy photographs
        available for purchase for study purposes only.
        Virtually every object photographed. Color slides
        available at $1.50-$3.00 each, more if new photography
        required.

                              * * *

WI133 PIONEER VILLAGE

        Hawthorne Hills County Park
        P. O. Box 206
        Cedarburg, WI 53012
        (414) 377-4510

        Alice Wendt
        Staff: 1 permanent, 6 volunteer

WI133 (Pioneer Village)
cont. Administered by the Ozaukee County Historical Society.

Museum village of restored and reconstructed buildings,
about 90% of which pertain to the area's German
settlers. Relevant buildings include Antone Rausch
Barn (1855), Bruno Woldt Blacksmith Shop (1850),
Hashek Log Hay Barn (1865), summer kitchen (1848),
log smoke house (1860's), Michael Ahner Log House
(1850), Steinke House (1860's), Ernst Gollnick Stone
Smoke House (1865), Karl Zettler Half-Timber House
(1849), Draiger House (1847), Stoney Hill School.
Buildings appropriately furnished. Private collection
of over 1000 photographs of old Cedarburg available
to Society for use by schools, groups, tours, etc.

Dates: 1840-1930.

100% cataloged; 50% photographed; library.

Hours: June--mid-Oct T 8-4. Appointment necessary
for research. Anyone may use research facilities.
Admission fee adult $1.75, children 6-16 50¢, children
under 6 and Society members free.

No loans.

                           * * *

WI134 OLD WORLD WISCONSIN

Route 1
P. O. Box 12-A
Eagle, WI 53119
(414) 594-2116

John Harbour, Director
Staff: 36 permanent, 30 seasonal

Museum village illustrating the lives of Wisconsin's
settlers; Germans constitute a major group. Collections include buildings, bedding, furniture, lighting
devices, clothing, adornments, toilet articles, agricultural tools, food processing and service articles,
housekeeping tools, musical instruments, textileworking tools, woodworking tools, other tools, transport,
decorative arts, games, toys, containers.

Dates: 1840-1915.

95% cataloged; 25% photographed; library.

Hours: Sat&Sun 9-5. Appointment necessary for
research. Resources available to public. Admission
charged.

Lends items for study and exhibit.

Cf. KOEPSEL HOUSE, WI251.
    CHRISTIAN TURCK HOUSE, WI252.

                           * * *

                                              Wisconsin

WI135 STATE HISTORICAL SOCIETY OF WISCONSIN
      Iconographic Collections
      (Visual and Recorded Sound Collections)

      816 State Street
      Madison, WI 53706
      (608) 262-9581

      Christine Schelshorn, Archivist, Iconographic
       Collections
      Staff: 3 permanent, 13 part-time

      Huge collection of broadsides, ephemera, and historical
      photographs of Germans in Wisconsin including portraits,
      brewing industry, business and industry, agriculture,
      organizations. Copyprints indicating material in
      family collections of local historical societies
      around Wisconsin. Krueger Collection of Pomeranian
      material from Watertown. Much material readily
      accessible but research will yield much more; check
      Name File, Place File, folders on brewing industry and
      textile manufacture.

      Dates: 19th and 20th centuries.

      Library.

      Hours: M-F 8-5. No appointment necessary. Resources
      available to the public. No admission or research
      fees.

      No loans. Write Iconographic Collections for current
      Service and Reproduction Fee Schedule.

                              * * *

WI136 FREISTADT HISTORICAL SOCIETY

      Trinity Lutheran Church
      10729 West Freistadt Road
      Mequon, WI 53092
      (414) 242-2045

      LeRoy Boehlke, Archives Committee
      Staff: 1 volunteer

      Area settled by Prussian Lutherans in 1839. The
      Historical Society is primarily an archive (immigra-
      tion materials, church books, passenger lists), but
      also has jurisdiction over a log cabin and fachwerk
      barn.

      Dates: 1839-1845.

      75% cataloged; no library.

      Hours: By appointment only. Anyone may use research
      facilities. No admission fee.

      No loans.

                              * * *

WI137 MILWAUKEE COUNTY HISTORICAL SOCIETY

>910 North Third Street
>Milwaukee, WI   53203
>(414) 273-8288

>Thomas M. Sersha, Curator of Collections
>Staff: 7 permanent, 2 volunteer

>Collections include bedding, furniture, adornments,
>clothing, toilet articles, agricultural tools, food
>processing and service articles, housekeeping tools,
>musical instruments, woodworking tools, brewing equip-
>ment, decorative arts, toys. An exhibit on Milwaukee
>brewing is in preparation (1978).

>Dates: 1837-1950.

>10% cataloged; 0% photographed; library.

>Hours: M-Sat 9-5, Sun 1-5. Appointment necessary.
>Resources available to general public. No admission
>or research fees.

>Lends articles. See Guide to German-American Research
>Materials in the Milwaukee County Historical Society,
>$3.00.

* * *

WI138 MILWAUKEE PUBLIC MUSEUM

>800 West Wells Street
>Milwaukee, WI   53233

>●History Division
>(414) 278-2768

>Dr. Lazar Brkich
>Betsy Kirchner
>Staff: 3 permanent

>General collection includes bedding, furniture,
>lighting devices, adornments, clothing, toilet articles,
>agricultural tools, food processing and service
>articles, housekeeping tools, other tools, transport,
>fractur, decorative arts, games, toys, containers.
>European Village, scheduled to open in December, 1979,
>will include representation of 19th-century German
>peasant home.

>Dates: 1700-present.
>98% cataloged; library.

>Hours: Daily 9-4:45. Appointment necessary to view
>articles in storage and to use library. General
>collection open to public. Admission fee for museum,
>none for library.

>Lends materials for special exhibits.

- - -

Wisconsin

WI138 (Milwaukee Public Museum--Photographic Department)
cont. ●Photographic Department
       (414) 278-2756

Janice L. Mahlberg, Photographer
Staff: 3 permanent, 1 volunteer

Approximately 10% of large collection (total of
300,000 articles) pertains to German-Americans.
Topics: history of Milwaukee, events, historic sites,
and artifacts.

Dates: late 1800's-early 1900's.

98% cataloged; library.

Hours: Daily 9-4:30. Appointment necessary.
Facilities available to public. No admission or
research fees.

Lends articles for study and special exhibits.

                            * * *

WI139 SWISS HISTORICAL VILLAGE   mail:
       West End of Sixth Avenue   c/o Paul Grossenbacher
       New Glarus, WI 53574   P. O. Box 445
       (608) 527-2317   New Glarus, WI   53573

Paul Grossenbacher, President
Staff: 15 permanent

Affiliated with the New Glarus Historical Society.

Museum village depicting lives of Swiss settlers.
Buildings include houses, sheds, log cabins, log
church, print shop, school, cheese factory, store.
Collections include food processing and service
articles, other tools, decorative arts.

Dates: 1845-1900.

75% cataloged; 75% photographed; small library.

Hours: May 1-Nov 1 daily 9-5. Appointment necessary
for research. Resources available mostly to students
and scholars. Admission fee adult $2.00, children
50¢ for guided tour.

No loans.

                            * * *

WI140 NEW HOLSTEIN HISTORICAL SOCIETY, INC.

       2103 Main Street
       New Holstein, WI 53061
       (414) 898-4377

Mrs. Pearl Muenster, President
Mrs. Hartwell J. Paul, Secretary
Staff: 12 directors, 20 volunteer

                                              Wisconsin

WI140 (New Holstein Historical Society, Inc.)
cont.
       Museum holdings reflect German settlement of New
       Holstein (1848). Society maintains Timm House (1893),
       William Ree Cabin (1857). Large collection includes
       bedding, furniture, lighting devices, adornments,
       clothing, toilet articles, agricultural tools, food
       processing and service articles, housekeeping tools,
       musical instruments, textileworking tools, woodworking
       tools, other tools, fractur, decorative arts, games,
       toys, containers.

       Dates: 1848-present.

       100% cataloged; 0% photographed; library.

       Hours: June-Sep, 2nd & 4th Sun 1:30-5. Appointment
       necessary. Resources open to public. No admission or
       research fees, but donations appreciated.

       No loans.

                           * * *

WI141 WATERTOWN HISTORICAL SOCIETY

       919 Charles Street
       Watertown, WI 53904
       (414) 261-2796

       Gladys Mollart, Curator
       Staff: 2 managers, 6 guides; 20 volunteer (gift shop)

       Restored First Kindergarten Building houses period
       furniture and artifacts. Kindergarten opened in 1856
       under Margarethe Meyer Schurz, wife of Carl Schurz and
       student of Froebel. Historical photographs: organi-
       zations, street scenes, business & industry, land
       transport, portraits, architecture, festivals, schools.

       Dates: 1852-1920.

       Hours: Apr-Oct daily 10-5. Appointment necessary
       for research. Resources available to public. General
       admission fee to all properties of the Historical
       Society.

       Lends materials, but rarely.

       The First Kindergarten Building is a National Register
       Site.
                           * * *

WI142 H. H. BENNETT STUDIO, INC.

       P. O. Box 145
       Wisconsin Dells, WI   53965
       (608) 253-2261

       Jean Reese, Manager
       Staff: 1 permanent part-time

                                                    Wisconsin

WI142 (H. H. Bennett Studio, Inc.)
cont. Collection of historical photographs of Wisconsin,
       especially the Wisconsin Dells (formerly Kilbourn)
       area. Included are photographs of the famous Milwaukee
       breweries and other German-American industries and
       businesses; churches, street scenes of German-American
       neighborhoods; portraits.

       Dates: 1880-1905.

       85% cataloged, not cataloged by ethnic group; no
       library.

       Hours: May-Oct 9-9. Appointment necessary. No
       admission or research fees.

       Articles lent for study and exhibits.
                                * * *

MB143 MENNONITE VILLAGE MUSEUM

       P. O. Box 1136
       Steinbach, Manitoba ROA 2AO
       (204) 326-9661

       Margaret Sinclair, Office Manager
       Staff: 25-30 volunteer (summers only)

       Affiliated with the Manitoba Mennonite Historical
       Society.

       Pioneer museum village depicting the lives of the
       early Mennonite settlers. Complex includes restored
       and reconstructed farmstead (house-barn), smithy,
       windmill, store, church, school. Collections (housed
       in 1882 log house) include bedding, furniture, lighting
       devices, adornments, clothing, toilet articles, agri-
       cultural tools, food processing and service articles,
       housekeeping tools, musical instruments, textileworking
       tools, woodworking tools, other tools, fractur or
       similar documents, transport, decorative arts, toys,
       containers.

       Dates: 1700-present.

       60% cataloged; 25% photographed; library.

       Hours: May 9-5, June 9-6, July-Aug 9-8, Sep 9-5.
       Appointment recommended for research. Resources
       available to public. Admission $1.50 for museum,
       includes use of library.

       Lends articles on special occasions.
                                * * *

NS144 PARKDALE-MAPLEWOOD COMMUNITY MUSEUM

       Barss Corners
       R. R. #1
       Maplewood, Nova Scotia
       (902) 644-2790
                                       Wisconsin-Nova Scotia

NS144 (Parkdale-Maplewood Community Museum)
cont.
Mrs. Lloyd F. Wentzel, Curator
Staff: 1-3 permanent (summers only), 5 volunteer

Many German immigrants entered Canada through Halifax
and the population of Lunenburg County is still mostly
of German extraction. Collections at the Parkdale-
Maplewood Museum include bedding, furniture, lighting
devices, adornments, clothing, toilet articles, agricultural tools, food processing and service articles,
housekeeping tools, musical instruments, textileworking
tools, woodworking tools, other tools, games, toys,
containers.

Dates: 1800-1920.

90% cataloged; 0% photographed; no library.

Hours: Summers only daily 1-5. No appointment
necessary during summer. Resources available to public.
No admission or research fees.

Loans made to special exhibits only.

* * *

ON145 JORDAN HISTORICAL MUSEUM OF THE TWENTY

Highway 8
P. O. Box 29
Jordan, Ontario L0R 1S0
(416) 562-5242

Harry Crowfoot, Director
Staff: 1 permanent, 2 volunteer

Museum consists of Vintage House (built by a Pennsylvania German immigrant ca. 1850), School House (1859),
Jacob Frye House (1815), and Mennonite churchyard.
Collections include bedding, furniture, lighting
devices, clothing, agricultural tools, food processing
and service articles, textileworking tools, woodworking
tools, other tools, decorative arts, toys, fractur,
containers.

Dates: 1795-1900.

100% cataloged; 0% photographed; no library.

Hours: Mid-May--Oct 12-6 daily. Appointment necessary
for research. Resources available to public. No
admission or research fees.

No loans.

* * *

ON146 DOON PIONEER VILLAGE

R. R. #2
Freeway Exit Interchange 34
Kitchener, Ontario N2G 3W5
(519) 893-4020

ON146 (Doon Pioneer Village)
cont.
       Alfred J. K. Schenk, Curator
       Staff: 6 permanent, volunteers from local organiza-
       tions

       Governed by the Grand River Conservation Authority.

       Pioneer village museum of 28 restored and reconstructed
       structures depicting the lives of native peoples and
       Pennsylvania German and Scottish settlers in the
       Waterloo/Kitchener area. German-Canadian materials
       include three houses (1830, 1840, 1840), two barns,
       one wagon shed (1890), blacksmith shop (1840), and
       print shop (1890); bedding, furniture, lighting
       devices, adornments, clothing, toilet articles, agri-
       cultural tools, food processing and service articles,
       housekeeping tools, musical instruments, textileworking
       tools, woodworking tools, fractur, land transport
       (including Conestoga wagon), bibles, decorative arts,
       games, toys, containers.

       Dates: ca. 1800-1900.

       25% cataloged; 0% photographed; library.

       Hours: May-Oct 10-5. Appointment necessary for
       research. Museum collections open to public. General
       admission charge for village; no charge for use of
       library.

       Loans made under special circumstances.
                              * * *

ON147 JOSEPH SCHNEIDER HOUSE

       466 Queen Street South
       Kitchener, Ontario
       no phone

       Mrs. H. Manley

       Governed by the Waterloo Regional Heritage Foundation.

       Foundation has undertaken restoration of this house,
       oldest in Kitchener (1820). Report on feasibility
       study, plans for restoration, floor plans, elevations,
       etc., may be obtained upon application to Foundation.
                              * * *

ON148 MARKHAM DISTRICT HISTORICAL MUSEUM

       Highway 48
       Markham, Ontario L3P 3J3
       (416) 294-4576

       John Lunau, Curator
       Mary Champion, Assistant Curator
       Staff: 2 permanent, 2 volunteer

       Owned and maintained by the Town of Markham.

                                                   Ontario

ON148   (Markham District Historical Museum)
cont.
        Historical museum of early life in the Markham area.
        1846 log home with period furnishings and early
        Mennonite home. Collection includes bedding, furni-
        ture, lighting devices, adornments, clothing, toilet
        articles, agricultural tools, food processing and
        service articles, housekeeping tools, musical instru-
        ments, textileworking tools, woodworking tools, other
        tools, fractur, transport, decorative arts, toys.
        Many items pertain to area's "Berczy" settlers.

        Dates: 1792-present.

        100% cataloged; no library.

        Hours: June 15-Sep 15 T-Sun 1-5, Sep 16-June 14 W-Sun
        1-5. Appointment necessary for research. Resources
        open to public. Admission fee charged.

        No loans.

                            * * *

ON149   BLACK CREEK PIONEER VILLAGE
                                         mail:
        Steeles Avenue at Jane Street   5 Shoreham Drive
        (1000 Murray Ross Parkway)   Downsview, Ont. M3N 1S4
        Toronto, Ontario
        (416) 661-6600

        Russell K. Cooper, Administrator
        Staff: 25 permanent

        Governed by the Metropolitan Toronto & Region Conser-
        vation Authority.

        Pioneer village museum of thirty buildings illustrating
        settlement in Ontario by a number of immigrant groups,
        including Germans and Pennsylvania Germans. German-
        Canadian structures include three residences (1816,
        1832, 1830's), two barns (1809,1825), backhouse
        (1820's), drive shed, apple storage cellar (1850's),
        cider mill (1840), piggery (1820's), slaughterhouse
        (1860's), Mennonite Meeting House (1825), town hall
        (1858). Collections also include furniture, agricul-
        tural tools, food processing and service articles,
        housekeeping tools, fractur, bibles, land transport.

        Dates: ca. 1810-1860's.

        Library.

        Hours: Apr-June, Sep-Oct 9:30-5; July-Aug 10-6; Nov-
        Jan 9:30-4; weekends & holidays: Apr-Oct 10-6; Nov-
        Jan 10-4:30. No appointment necessary to use collec-
        tions, necessary for use of library. General admission
        fee for museum, none for library.

        Materials lent occasionally.

                            * * *

                                                     Ontario

SK150 ST. PETER'S ABBEY ARCHIVES

P. O. Box 10
Muenster, Saskatchewan SOK 2YO
(306) 682-3373

Bede Hubbard, O. S. B., Archivist
Staff: 1 permanent

Historical photographs of German settlers in the
Muenster area; bibles.

Dates: 19th & 20th centuries.

100% cataloged; library.

Hours: 9-12, 1-5 daily. Appointment recommended.
Anyone may use research facilities. No research fees.

Lends articles for study and special exhibits.

                          * * *

SK151 STRASBOURG MUSEUM

P. O. Box 446
Strasbourg, Saskatchewan SOG 4VO
no phone

Crystal Hey
Staff: 1 permanent

Small number of German-Canadian artifacts including
lighting devices, adornments, toilet articles, food
processing and service articles, housekeeping tools,
musical instruments.

Dates: 1890-1940.

95% cataloged; 0% photographed.

Hours: F-T 2-8. No appointment necessary. Resources
open to public. No admission or research fees.

No loans.

                          * * *

SK152 WESTERN DEVELOPMENT MUSEUM
      Yorkton Branch   Saskatoon Branch

Highway 14 West   2610 Lorne Avenue South
P. O. Box 1033   P. O. Box 1910
Yorkton, Sask. S7N 2X3   Saskatoon, Sask. S7K 3S5
(306) 783-8361   (306) 652-1910

Ruth Bitner, Collections Co-ordinator (Saskatoon)
Jack Zepp, Manager, Yorkton Branch
Staff: 23 permanent, 50 volunteer

The Western Development Museum is a network of four
branches (at North Battleford, Saskatoon, Yorkton, and
Moose Jaw) in the province depicting Saskatchewan's
history. The Yorkton branch concentrates on the

                                    Saskatchewan

SK152 (Western Development Museum--Yorkton Branch)
cont. multi-cultural heritage of Saskatchewan, including
       German-Canadians. German-Canadian holdings include
       agricultural tools, armaments, musical instruments,
       clocks, toys.

       Dates: 19th century.

       75% cataloged; inventory being computerized; 5%
       photographed; library at Saskatoon.

       Hours: Summer 9-9 daily: winter M-F 9-5, Sat&Sun 12-5.
       Office hours in Saskatoon: M-F 8:30-5. Appointment
       necessary for research. Resources available to
       serious students. Admission adult $1.50, no library
       use fee.

       Lends pieces to other museums under certain conditions.

                            * * *

Chapter II:

NATIONAL REGISTER SITES

This chapter describes National Register sites of German-American significance. The entries were abstracted from the 1976 edition of the <u>National Register of Historic Places</u>, which is complete through the end of 1974. At present the Canadian National Historic Parks and Sites list does not include enough places of German-Canadian significance to warrant a search.

Cross-references to other entries are indicated where a direct overlap or correspondence of holdings exists, or where the entries are very closely related.

CA153 SUTTER'S FORT

2701 L Street
Sacramento, CA 95816

1839-1844

Fort includes living quarters, barracks, stables,
granary, store, kitchens, and workshops enclosed
within adobe walls; reconstructed, 1891-1893.
Established 1839 as fortified settlement by one of
state's earliest settlers, John Sutter (German immigrant), rancher, fur trader, and landholder; served as
way station for wagon trains on California section of
Oregon Trail; became economic, political and social
center of the only settled portion of state's interior.

State-owned.

National Historic Landmark.

* * *

CA154 CHARLES KRUG WINERY

St. Helena Highway
St. Helena, CA 94574

1861

Oldest operating winery in Napa Valley, built for
pioneer winemaker Charles Krug, who made first commercial wine in Napa County, 1858; illustrates winemaking
process.

Private.

* * *

CA155 RHINE HOUSE

2000 Main Street
St. Helena, CA 94574

1883

Built as replica of owner Frederick Beringer's house
in Mainz, Germany; serves winery established by German
immigrants in mid-19th century; 1000 feet of cellars
on hill beyond home. Stone; half-timbered upper floor.

Private.

* * *

GA156 EBENEZER TOWNSITE AND JERUSALEM LUTHERAN CHURCH

State Route 275
near Springfield, GA 31329

ca. 1736

Church and cemetery are all that remain of first
permanent settlement of Georgia's second group of
colonists, who emigrated from Salzburg to avoid Roman

GA156 (Ebenezer Townsite and Jerusalem Lutheran Church)
cont.
       Catholic persecution. Most notable resident was John
       Adam Treutlen, state's first governor under its
       constitution. Steadily declined after 1800.

       Private.

                             * * *

IL157 GUERTLER HOUSE

       101 Blair Street
       Alton, IL 62002

       ca. 1850

       Home of Ignaz Bruch, early stone mason and German
       immigrant.

       Public/private.

                             * * *

IN158 ATHENAEUM (DAS DEUTSCHE HAUS)

       401 East Michigan Street
       Indianapolis, IN 46204

       1893-1894

       Large recreation and social club in German part of
       Indianapolis, which had expanded greatly with new
       immigration in 1880's and 1890's.

       Private.

                             * * *

IN159 NEW HARMONY HISTORIC DISTRICT

       New Harmony, IN 47631

       19th century

       District containing about 35 restored buildings,
       mostly of brick, associated with both Rappite and
       Owenite communal experiments. Founded and build as
       self-sufficient community, Harmony, in 1815 by the
       Rappites, German religious refugees led by George Rapp;
       purchased and renamed New Harmony in 1825 by Robert
       Owen, British industrialist, social critic, and
       Utopian.

       Multiple public/private.

       National Historic Landmark.
       Historic American Buildings Survey.

       Cf. HISTORIC NEW HARMONY, INC., IN16.
           NEW HARMONY STATE MEMORIAL, IN17,
           WORKINGMEN'S INSTITUTE LIBRARY & MUSEUM, IN18,
           OLD ECONOMY VILLAGE, PA79.

                             * * *

IA160 FRICK'S TAVERN

   1402-1404 West Third Street
   Davenport, IA   52802

   ca. 1870's

   Served as social center for city's German residents
   for over a century.

   Private.

                              * * *

IA161 JACOB WENTZ HOUSE

   219 North Gilbert Street
   Iowa City, IA   52240

   1847

   Built for German immigrant shoemaker, Jacob Wentz.
   Only remaining two-story native stone house from
   original town.

   Private; not accessible to the public.

                              * * *

IA162 AMANA VILLAGES

   near Middle Amana, IA   52203

   1855

   Area includes seven villages founded by communal
   religious society; kitchen, shops, mills, and
   factories, later held in common by the society in the
   late-19th century. Organized by German pietists under
   the leadership of Christian Metz; sect settled near
   Buffalo, New York, in 1842, migrated to Iowa in 1854.
   One of the most successful Utopian settlements of 19th-
   century America, the Amana Society reorganized as a
   joint stock company in 1932 and continues to operate
   today.

   Multiple public/private.

   National Historic Landmark.

   Historic American Buildings Survey.

   Cf. MUSEUM OF AMANA HISTORY, IA19.

                              * * *

KS163 MUELLER-SCHMIDT HOUSE

   112 East Vine Street
   Dodge City, KS   67801

   1879-1880

   Fine provincial house built for bootmaker John Mueller;
   later owned by German-born blacksmith Adam Schmidt.

   Owned by Ford County.

                              * * *
                                        Iowa-Kansas (Sites)

KS164 BERNHARD WARKENTIN HOMESTEAD

North of Halstead, KS   67056

1870's-1880's

Farm complex includes house, barn, chicken barn, hog
barn, powerhouse, and silo. Homestead established by
Russian-German immigrant, Bernhard Warkentin, one of
the early producers, experimenters, promoters, and
millers of Turkey Red winter wheat. His introduction
of this wheat and encouragement of Mennonite immigrants
were largely responsible for making Kansas the
"breadbasket" of the nation.

Private.

Cf. WARKENTIN MILL, KS166.

* * *

KS165 CHRISTIAN WETZEL CABIN

Jct. I-70 and State Route 57
near Junction City, KS   66441

1857

During Wetzel family ownership (1860-1864), this was
site of first services of Lutheran Church/Missouri
Synod in Kansas.

Private.

* * *

KS166 WARKENTIN MILL

Third and Main Streets
Newton, KS   67114

1879

Purchased in 1886 by Bernhard Warkentin.

Private; not accessible to the public.

Cf. BERNHARD WARKENTIN HOMESTEAD, KS164.

* * *

KS167 DIETRICH CABIN

Ottawa City Park
Ottawa, KS   66067

1859

One of Kansas' few remaining early log cabins; built
by German immigrant Jacob Dietrich.

Owned by Franklin County.

* * *

KS168 ST. FIDELIS CATHOLIC CHURCH

SE Corner of St. Anthony & Delaware Streets
Victoria, KS 67671

1908-1911

Romanesque/Renaissance Revival church. Serves area's
Catholic Germans from Russia.

* * *

ME169 GERMAN CHURCH AND CEMETERY

Maine Route 32
south of Waldoboro, ME 04572

1772

Built to serve German settlement founded in 1753;
abandoned when sermons continued to be delivered in
German to an almost exclusively English-speaking
congregation.

Private.

Historic American Buildings Survey.

* * *

MD170 AMERICAN BREWERY (WEISSNER BREWERY)

1701 North Gay Street
Baltimore, MD 21213

1887

Built to accommodate growing production of one of city's
more successful breweries, established by John
Frederick Weissner, 1863.

Private.

Historic American Engineering Record.

* * *

MD171 OTTERBEIN CHURCH

112 West Conway Street
Baltimore, MD 21201

1785-1786

Restored. Site of first Conference of United Brethren
in Christ. City's only 18th-century church in contin-
uous use.

Private.

Historic American Buildings Survey.

* * *

MD172 SCHEIFFERSTADT

West Second and Rosemont Streets
Frederick, MD 21701

MD172 (Scheifferstadt)
cont.   Mid-18th century

Excellent example of early area construction features
half-timbered construction and unique framing system;
reflects German and other European influences. Home
of Josef Brunner, early German immigrant.

Private; not accessible to the public.

* * *

MD173 AMELUNG HOUSE AND GLASSWORKS

Off U. S. Route 240
southwest of Urbana, MD

1785-1795

No aboveground remains of factory; archaeological
investigation by Corning Museum, Smithsonian Institution, and Colonial Williamsburg, 1962-1963. Built for
Johann Friedrich Amelung, whose glassworks was one of
America's first factories.

Private; not accessible to the public.

Historic American Buildings Survey.

* * *

MI174 INDIAN MISSION

590 East Bay Street
Sebewaing, MI   48759

1849

Mission house, chapel, and school for Chippewa Indians;
built by German missionary John J. Auch, for whom town
was originally named (Auchville).

Private.

* * *

MN175 SEPPMAN MILL

Minnesota Route 68
Minneopa State Park
near Mankato, MN   56001

1862-1863

One of few wind-powered mills in state; built by
German immigrant Louis Seppman.

State-owned.

* * *

MN176 FEDERAL POST OFFICE BUILDING

Center Street & Broadway
New Ulm, MN   56073

1909-1910

MN176   (Federal Post Office Building)
cont.
         Brick and terra cotta, 1½ stories. Design similar to
         the English High Victorian "Pont Street Dutch" work
         of the late-19th century. Reflects European background
         of settlers.

         Federal/United States Postal Service.

         Cf. BROWN COUNTY HISTORICAL SOCIETY, MN35.

                              * * *

MN177 HERMANN MONUMENT

         Hermann Heights Park
         New Ulm, MN   56073

         1888-1897

         Dome and statue created by Alfonz Pelzl and Julius
         Berndt. Thirty-two-foot statue (above dome) of Hermann
         of the Cherusci tribe, leader who unified German tribes
         in 9 A. D. and drove Roman legions back to Rhine River.
         Symbol of German immigration to the United States.

         Municipal.

         Cf. BROWN COUNTY HISTORICAL SOCIETY, MN35.

                              * * *

MN178 KIESLING HOUSE

         220 North Minnesota Street
         New Ulm, MN   56073

         Pre-1862

         One of few buildings from first decade of town's
         founding; served as defensive outpost during 1862
         Sioux Indian War.

         Municipal.

         Cf. BROWN COUNTY HISTORICAL SOCIETY, MN35

                              * * *

MN179 MELGES BAKERY

         213 South Minnesota Street
         New Ulm, MN   56073

         1865

         Operated as bakery by Frederick G. Melges, 1871-1891.

         County-owned.

         Cf. BROWN COUNTY HISTORICAL SOCIETY, MN35.

                              * * *

MN180 AUGUST SCHELL BREWING COMPANY

20th Street South
New Ulm, MN 56073

Late-19th century

Five-building brewery complex with original 1860 brick
building which served as first residence and brewery.
With exception of house, buildings are simple industrial structures. Machinery includes functioning
refrigeration compressor patented in 1884. Sole
surviving of seven breweries in New Ulm; established
1860 by German immigrant, August Schell, in whose
family it still operates.

Private.

Cf. BROWN COUNTY HISTORICAL SOCIETY, MN35.

* * *

MN181 WENDELIN GRIMM HOMESTEAD

Carver Park Reserve
near St. Bonifacius, MN 55375

Mid-late 19th century

Homestead of German immigrant Wendelin Grimm, who
developed the first hardy winter strain of alfalfa,
which became a valuable crop in early-20th century.

County-owned.

* * *

MN182 SHAKOPEE HISTORIC DISTRICT

Memorial Park
Shakopee, MN 55379

Prehistoric-19th century

Restoration in process to create a period community.

County-owned.

Cf. MURPHY'S LANDING, MN37.

* * *

MO183 BETHEL HISTORIC DISTRICT

Bethel, MO 63434

19th century

Community containing 50 buildings, 18 of which are
related to 19th-century religious communal society.
The largely German Society of Bethel was founded in
1844 and led by William Keil; upon Keil's death in
1877, Bethel broke ties with sister society in Oregon
and disbanded. Town incorporated 1883.

Minnesota-Missouri (Sites)

MO183 (Bethel Historic District)
cont.   Multiple private.

    Cf. ELIM, MO184.
        AURORA COLONY HISTORIC DISTRICT, OR209.
        JOHN STAUFFER HOUSE AND BARN, OR210.

* * *

MO184 ELIM (DR. WILLIAM KEIL HOUSE)

    east of Bethel, MO   63434

    Late 1840's

    Built for William Keil, German immigrant founder of
    Society of Bethel, 19th-century communal society.

    Private; not accessible to the public.

    Cf. BETHEL HISTORIC DISTRICT, MO183.
        AURORA COLONY HISTORIC DISTRICT, OR209.
        JOHN STAUFFER HOUSE AND BARN, OR210.

* * *

MO185 HERMANN HISTORIC DISTRICT

    Hermann, MO   65041

    19th century

    Approximately 13 blocks of old Hermann; contains
    numerous commercial and residential structures, the
    majority of which are brick. Common are commercial
    buildings with residential quarters above or behind
    business floors. Hermann was planned and settled in
    the 1830's by the German Settlement Society of Phila-
    delphia. For information regarding the Pommer-Gentner
    House, the Strehly House, and the Dr. Feldman House,
    contact Martin E. Shay, Site Administrator, Deutschheim
    State Historic Site, 109 West Second Street, Hermann,
    Missouri 65041.

    Multiple public/private.

    Historic American Buildings Survey.

    Cf. HISTORIC HERMANN, INC., MO40.
        OLD STONE HILL HISTORIC DISTRICT, MO186.

* * *

MO186 OLD STONE HILL HISTORIC DISTRICT

    Hermann, MO   65041

    1869-1920

    Self-sufficient wine-producing complex. Established
    1847 by Michael Poeschel, the Stone Hill Wine Company
    became the third largest wine-producing company in
    the world. Prohibition caused the operation to close
    in 1920; business recently resumed.

Missouri (Sites)

MO186   (Old Stone Hill Historic District)
cont.   Private.

        Cf. HISTORIC HERMANN MUSEUM & RIVER ROOM, MO40.
        HERMANN HISTORIC DISTRICT, MO185.

* * *

MO187   BORGMANN MILL

        County Road D
        Marthasville, MO   63357

        ca. 1850

        Built by Frederick Wilhelm Borgmann. Unusual Dutch
        door. Handcarved wooden milling machinery, still in
        good condition, includes perhaps the only extant
        barley huller and corn grinder in the Midwest con-
        structed entirely of wood. One of a small number of
        wooden mills built; used only briefly in the mid-
        nineteenth century.

        Private; not accessible to the public.

* * *

MO188   ANHEUSER-BUSCH BREWERY

        721 Pestalozzi Street
        St. Louis, MO   63118

        Mid-19th century

        Brewery complex containing 158 manufacturing and ware-
        house buildings over 70-block area. Adolphus Busch
        expanded small brewery into internationally renowned
        business, and pioneered in methods of pasteurization
        and refrigerated shipping and storage.

        Private.

        National Historic Landmark.

* * *

MT189   GRANT-KOHRS RANCH NATIONAL HISTORIC SITE

        Deer Lodge, MT   59722

        1863

        Ranch complex includes two-story frame and brick ranch
        house (1863, 1890), several log cabins (late 1850's-
        1860's), other frame outbuildings, old corrals, and
        some ranching equipment. Established by John Grant,
        first major stockman in the region, 1863: bought and
        enlarged by Conrad Kohrs, Montana cattle baron, in
        1866. Preserved as working ranch.

        Federal/National Park Service/non-federal.

* * *

MT190 KLUGE HOUSE

> 540 West Main Street
> Helena, MT 59601
>
> 1880's
>
> Rare American example of Prussian 17th-19th century building construction. Built by German immigrant Emil Kluge. Hewn-log first floor, open timber frame second story.
>
> Private.
>
> Historic American Buildings Survey.

* * *

NE191 EMMANUEL LUTHERAN CHURCH

> 1500 Hickory Street
> Dakota City, NE 68731
>
> 1860
>
> Reputedly territory's first Lutheran church.
>
> Municipal.
>
> Historic American Buildings Survey.

* * *

NE192 STOLLEY STATE PARK HISTORIC DISTRICT

> Stolley State Park
> Grand Island, NE 68801
>
> 19th century
>
> Log residence of county's first settler, William Stolley; reconstructed log cabin; county's first public school buildings; site of fortified blockhouse called Fort Independence; and an unidentified small frame structure, survival of settlement founded by German immigrants in 1857 under the leadership of William Stolley.
>
> State-owned.

* * *

NJ193 MORAVIAN CHURCH

> Swedesboro-Sharptown Road
> Oliphant's Mill, NJ 08055
>
> ca. 1789
>
> Oldest and only surviving Moravian church building in southern New Jersey; design attributed to Francis Boehler, Moravian minister.
>
> Private.
>
> Historic American Buildings Survey.

* * *

NM194 SPIEGELBERG HOUSE (SPITZ HOUSE)

   237 East Palace Street
   Santa Fe, NM 87501

   1880

   Built for Willi Spiegelberg by European artisans;
   traditional regional building material used with
   eastern architectural form.

   Private.

                            * * *

NY195 FORT HERKIMER CHURCH (REFORMED PROTESTANT DUTCH CHURCH
       OF GERMAN FLATS)

   State Route 5S
   East Herkimer, NY 13350

   1767

   Built by Palatine German settlers; part of fortification
   under command of Sir William Johnson during French and
   Indian War.

   Private.

   Historic American Buildings Survey.

                            * * *

NY196 PALATINE CHURCH

   Mohawk Turnpike
   Palatine, NY

   1770

   Georgian; altered. Built for pioneer German settlement.

   Private.

   Historic American Buildings Survey.

                            * * *

NC197 MICHAEL BRAUN HOUSE

   State Route 2308
   Granite Quarry, NC 28072

   1766

   Reflects 18th-century Pennsylvania German building
   techniques. Reputedly the county's oldest remaining
   dwelling.

   Private.

   Cf. ROWAN MUSEUM, INC. NC62.

                            * * *

NC198 WEIDNER ROCK HOUSE

> State Route 1142
> Hickory, NC 28601
>
> 1799
>
> Reflects German building style and techniques. Built
> by German immigrant from Pennsylvania, Henry Weidner,
> owned by family until 1804. Probably moved from
> original site and reconstructed 1844.
>
> Private; not accessible to the public.

* * *

NC199 GRACE EVANGELICAL AND REFORMED CHURCH

> Rockwell, NC 28138
>
> 1795
>
> One of two area churches that reflect 18th-century
> building techniques by German settlers from Pennsyl-
> vania. Housed German Presbyterian congregation.
>
> Private.

* * *

NC200 ZION LUTHERAN CHURCH (ORGAN CHURCH)

> State Route 1006
> Rockwell, NC 28138
>
> ca. 1794
>
> State's oldest example of Lutheran ecclesiastical
> architecture; built for members of the Zion Lutheran
> Church organized in 1745.
>
> Private.

* * *

NC201 BETHABARA MORAVIAN CHURCH

> 2147 Bethabara Road
> Winston-Salem, NC 27108
>
> 1788
>
> Built through efforts of Frederick William Marshall,
> distinguished Moravian clergyman; houses the earliest
> congregation of the Moravian Church, South.
>
> Private.
>
> Historic American Buildings Survey.
>
> Cf. HISTORIC BETHABARA, NC63.

* * *

North Carolina (Sites)

NC202 OLD SALEM HISTORIC DISTRICT

Salem College campus and area near Salem Square
Winston-Salem, NC 27108

ca. 1770

Well-preserved example of 18th-century colonial community; includes approximately 22 residential and
commercial buildings. Founded 1766 by Moravians from
Bethlehem, Pennsylvania; plan reflects influence of
mid-18th-century European town planning and architectural designs. Became trading center of Piedmont
region with strong emphasis on crafts and commerce;
stopping point for settlers moving westward. More
than half of original buildings survive; many still
serve original functions.

Private.

National Historic Landmark.
Historic American Buildings Survey.

Cf. OLD SALEM, INC., NC65.

* * *

NC203 SALEM TAVERN

800 South Main Street
Winston-Salem, NC 27108

1784

First brick structure built in Moravian settlement at
Salem; operated during town's period as trading center
for western North Carolina.

Private.

National Historic Landmark.

Cf. OLD SALEM, INC., NC65.

* * *

NC204 SINGLE BROTHERS' HOUSE

South Main and Academy Streets
Winston-Salem, NC 27108

1768

Traditional German half-timber construction. Earliest
major building still standing in Moravian community of
Old Salem. Used as dormitory and workshops for
apprentices, unmarried men after apprenticeship, and
master craftsmen.

Private.

National Historic Landmark.
Historic American Buildings Survey.

Cf. OLD SALEM, INC., NC65.

* * *

North Carolina (Sites)

NC205 ZEVELY HOUSE

   734 Oak Street
   Winston-Salem, NC   27108

   19th century

   Reputedly city's oldest remaining dwelling; home of
   Moravian cabinetmaker Vannimmen Zevely.

   Private; not accessible to the public.

   Cf. OLD SALEM, INC., NC65.

                        * * *

OH206 WALDSCHMIDT-CAMP DENNISON DISTRICT

   7509 and 7567 Glendale-Milford Road
   Cincinnati, OH   45242

   ca. 1805-1810

   Two similar buildings of coursed rubble mark the
   settlement of New Germany, established 1794 by group
   of German Pietists; state's oldest stone buildings.

   Private.

                        * * *

OH207 GERMAN VILLAGE

   Columbus, OH   43206

   1820-early-20th century

   Urban "village" district of 233 acres with over 1800
   structures, largely residences and commercial buildings.
   Much restoration work. German settlement directly
   south of central business district, settled throughout
   19th century with ethnic clubs, churches, school and
   newspaper; well-defined community architecturally and
   socially. Twentieth-century inroads on German Village
   culture and social life brought area decline, but
   since the formation of the German Village Society in
   1960, district has regained vitality. The Society
   guides restoration efforts, maintains a Center for
   Information at 624 South Third Street, Columbus, Ohio
   43206, and provides group tours and lectures.

   Multiple public/private.

                        * * *

OH208 GNADENHUTTEN MASSACRE SITE

   County Route 10
   Gnadenhutten, OH   44269

   1782

   Obelisk marks burial site of 90 Delaware Indians
   massacred at Gnadenhutten, a Moravian mission, in
   1782. The Moravians and the Indian converts remained

                              North Carolina-Ohio (Sites)

OH208 (Gnadenhutten Massacre Site)
cont.
        neutral during the Revolution, but following Shawnee
        raids in Pennsylvania, 150 militiamen killed all the
        Indians at the mission.

        State-owned.

                              * * *

OR209 AURORA COLONY HISTORIC DISTRICT

        Aurora, OR   97002

        1856-1881

        Contains 18 major structures including 16 dwellings, a
        restored meeting hall, a barn, and an octagonal out-
        building. Remains of the largest of four towns built
        in the west as part of a communal society founded by
        Dr. William Keil in the mid-19th century.

        Private.

        Cf. BETHEL HISTORIC DISTRICT, MO183.
            ELIM, MO184.
            JOHN STAUFFER HOUSE AND BARN, OR210.
                              * * *

OR210 JOHN STAUFFER HOUSE AND BARN

        Hubbard, OR   97032

        ca. 1865

        Log dwelling built by John Stauffer. One of six major
        structures remaining on area farms associated with
        Aurora, the largest and most successful of four
        Christian communal settlements founded by Prussian
        immigrant William Keil.

        Private.

        Cf. BETHEL HISTORIC DISTRICT, MO183.
            ELIM, MO184.
            AURORA COLONY HISTORIC DISTRICT, OR209.
                              * * *

PA211 PHILIP CHRISTMAN HOUSE

        Bally, PA   19503

        ca. 1750

        Rock-faced random ashlar, one story over basement,
        second-story front porch accessible only by bank into
        which house is built; food and animal storage basement
        features stream which acts as cooling device; outbuild-
        ings. Typical of early German structures built into
        mound slopes for additional protection from the elements
        and to provide more sound construction support and
        effective storage area.

        Private.

                      * * *   Ohio-Pennsylvania (Sites)

PA212 BETHLEHEM HISTORIC DISTRICT I, SUBDISTRICT A

Bethlehem, PA 18018

18th-19th centuries

Downtown district includes numerous commercial, residential, and industrial structures; noted for 18th-
century limestone buildings with canted gabled roofs
with Germanic influence. Founded in 1741 by Moravian
immigrants, Bethlehem was considered a remarkable
settlement for its early application of city planning
and civil engineering principles, its social amenities,
and for its self-sufficiency.

Multiple public/private.

Cf. OLD SALEM, INC., NC65.
    HISTORIC BETHLEHEM, INC., PA80.

* * *

PA213 GRISTMILLER'S HOUSE

459 Old York Road
Bethlehem, PA 18018

1782

House built to accommodate miller's family near community gristmill; illustrates adoption of exogenous
building techniques and styles in Moravian community.

Municipal.

Cf. HISTORIC BETHLEHEM, INC., PA80.

* * *

PA214 MORAVIAN SUN INN

564 Main Street
Bethlehem, PA 18018

1760

Constructed to serve travelers on the North-South route
between New England and the southern colonies; late-
18th-century visitors gathered here for guided tours
of the Moravian communal industrial complex. Housed
refugees from Philadelphia area following Battle of
the Brandywine.

Private.

Cf. MORAVIAN MUSEUMS OF BETHLEHEM, PA83.

* * *

PA215 OLD WATERWORKS

Bethlehem, PA 18018

1762

PA215 (Old Waterworks)
cont.
       Supplied water to community 90 feet above pumphouse;
       considered the first pumped or forced water system in
       the United States. Within Historic Subdistrict A.

       Municipal.

       Historic American Buildings Survey.

       Cf. HISTORIC BETHLEHEM, INC., PA80.
           BETHLEHEM HISTORIC DISTRICT I, SUBDISTRICT A, PA212.

                              * * *

PA216 KNURR LOG HOUSE

       Meng Road
       Delphi, PA

       ca. 1750

       Log construction, partially shingled, 1½ stories.
       Excellent example of Germanic log dwelling.

       Private; not accessible to public.

                              * * *

PA217 EVANSBURG HISTORIC DISTRICT (PROVIDENCE SQUARE)

       U. S. 422
       Evansburg, PA

       18th-19th centuries

       Small town district predominantly of two-story gabled
       roof stone houses and barns, many stuccoed, fine
       examples of area 18th- and early-19th-century construc-
       tion; cemetery, library building. Well-preserved area
       illustrating early settlement; includes location of
       cemetery and houses of Mennonite group that broke from
       strict church pacifist policy to pay Revolutionary War
       taxes.

       Multiple public/private.

                              * * *

PA218 KLEIN MEETINGHOUSE

       Maple Avenue
       Harleysville, PA 19438

       1843

       Frame, wide plank sheathing, 1 story; adjacent cemetery.
       Built for congregation of local Dunkards, also known
       as German Baptist Brethren, a group that settled in
       Pennsylvania in 1714.

       Private.

                              * * *

PA219 HARMONY HISTORIC DISTRICT

   State Route 68
   Harmony, PA 16037

   1805-1814

   Remains of community arranged around central square and
   surrounded by open space; contains brick structures
   illustrating area interpretation of late-Georgian
   elements. First communistic settlement of the Harmony
   Society, group of German Pietists, founded by George
   Rapp; developed into a successful agricultural and
   manufacturing community.

   Multiple public/private.

   National Historic Landmark.

   Cf. OLD ECONOMY VILLAGE, PA79.
       NEW HARMONY HISTORIC DISTRICT, IN159.
                          * * *

PA220 HOTTENSTEIN MANSION

   U. S. Route 222
   Kutztown, PA 19530

   1783

   Limestone, sandstone trim; 2½ stories; rear kitchen
   wing; outbuildings; excellent interior woodwork and
   examples of fractur.

   Private.
                          * * *

PA221 DIELMAN KOLB HOMESTEAD

   Kinsey Road
   Lederach, PA 19450

   18th century

   Fieldstone, 2½ stories. Similar to three-room plan
   Germanic houses common in the area in 18th century.
   Built by Dielman Kolb, early area settler. Summer
   kitchen.

   Private; not accessible to the public.
                          * * *

PA222 JULIUS STURGIS PRETZEL HOUSE

   219-221 East Main Street
   Lititz, PA 17543

   1784

   Stone, brick 2½ stories; brick factory added to rear
   1861; original factory equipment intact. First commercial pretzel factory in United States; started by

                                      Pennsylvania (Sites)

PA222 (Julius Sturgis Pretzel House)
cont.
     Julius Sturgis in 1861. Company moved to new building
     in 1951 and factory and house became restaurant/museum.

     Private.

                         * * *

PA223 KEIM HOMESTEAD

     Lobachsville, PA

     18th century

     Stone, 2½ stories; ca. 1750-1780. Small, earlier stone
     cabin on property constructed between 1706 and 1732
     by German immigrant Johannes Keim. Both illustrative
     of German influence in Pennsylvania architecture.

     Private.

     Historic American Buildings Survey.

                         * * *

PA224 JOHANNES EBERLY HOUSE (OLD BRICKER HOUSE)

     U. S. Route 11
     Mechanicsburg, PA 17055

     18th century

     Fieldstone, 2½ stories. Rural Germanic-English inter-
     pretation of Georgian-Federal elements. Home of
     Johannes Eberly, wealthy Mennonite farmer.

     Private; not accessible to the public.

                         * * *

PA225 HOUSE OF MILLER AT MILLBACH

     Newmanstown, PA 17073

     1752

     Limestone, 2½ stories; 1874 gabled mill addition; much
     of original interior work now at Philadelphia Museum
     of Art; log cabin on grounds. Substantial house/mill
     combination representative of German-influenced build-
     ing in state.

     Private.

     Cf. PHILADELPHIA MUSEUM OF ART, PA103.

                         * * *

PA226 ANDREAS RIETH HOMESTEAD

     Geryville Pike
     Pennsburg, PA 18073

     18th century

PA226 (Andreas Rieth Homestead)
cont.
       Stone, 2½-story main house, 1½-story barn with gabled
       roof. Both typical of early rural colonial construc-
       tion in state.

       Private.

                              * * *

PA227 BEGGARSTOWN SCHOOL

       6669 Germantown Avenue
       Philadelphia, PA 19144

       1740

       Stone 1½ stories; restored 1915. Early education
       building, typical of German parish schools of the time.

       Private.

                              * * *

PA228 COLONIAL GERMANTOWN HISTORIC DISTRICT

       Germantown Avenue
       Philadelphia, PA 19144

       19th-19th centuries

       Contains approximately 50 18th-century and very early-
       19th-century residences, churches, schools, and
       taverns. Founded in 1683 by immigrating Netherlanders
       and Germans fleeing religious persecution; developed
       predominantly by German immigrants who established
       religious and educational institutions, as well as an
       industrial economic base. Reflects the wide range of
       social, economic, and cultural interests which developed
       in an isolated community before the Revolution and in
       a more open one after the war.

       Private.

       National Historic Landmark.
       Historic American Buildings Survey.

       Cf. GERMANTOWN HISTORICAL SOCIETY, PA101.

                              * * *

PA229 MENNONITE MEETINGHOUSE

       6119 Germantown Avenue
       Philadelphia, PA 19144

       1770

       Stone, 1½ stories; 1909 addition; church interior
       restored 1952. Replaced original 1708 log meetinghouse
       where the first Mennonite congregation in America held
       regular services. Present communion table believed
       used for signing of 1688 Germantown Protest against

                                        Pennsylvania (Sites)

PA229 (Mennonite Meetinghouse)
cont.   slavery, first attempt by any group in British America
        to disapprove officially of slavery.

        Private.

        Historic American Buildings Survey.

                              * * *

PA230 BRENDLE FARMS

        Jct. State Routes 501 & 897
        Schaefferstown, PA 17088

        18th-19th centuries

        Three hundred forty-seven acre rural area encompassing
        stone and frame structures originally serving domestic
        and farm functions; includes stone "bank" houses with
        elements illustrating Swiss traditions carried to the
        New World, and one of the best built stone barns in
        the area.

        Multiple private.

        Cf. THOMAS R. BRENDLE MEMORIAL LIBRARY & MUSEUM, PA107.
        ALEXANDER SCHAEFFER FARM MUSEUM, PA108.

                              * * *

PA231 JOHN ENGLEHARDT HOMESTEAD

        Keyser Road
        near Schwenksville, PA 19473

        early-18th century

        Stone, stuccoed, 2½-story house and 1½-story stone
        barn. Buildings illustrating small rural homestead of
        18th-century Pennsylvania.

        Private; not accessible to the public.

                              * * *

PA232 CONRAD GRUBB HOMESTEAD

        Perkiomenville Road
        near Schwenksville, PA 19473

        1754

        Random rubble 2½-story house; brick addition; barn,
        milkhouse, shed, and wellhouse on lot; restored. Rural
        homestead built by weaver and farmer Conrad Grubb;
        house displays a variation of common area 3-room plan,
        originally derived from Germanic traditions.

        Private.

                              * * *

                                        Pennsylvania (Sites)

PA233 LONG MEADOW FARM (PLANK HOUSE AND BARN)

State Route 73
near Schwenksville, PA   19473

mid-18th century

Brick, stuccoed 2½-story house with 19th-century ell;
barn. Rural homestead illustrating combination of
traditional Germanic building approach and contemporary
English/American approach.

Private; not accessible to the public.

* * *

PA234 AUGUSTUS LUTHERAN CHURCH

Seventh Avenue East & Main Street
Trappe, PA

1743

Built under direction of Dr. Heinrich Melchior Muhlenberg, patriarch of the Lutheran Church in America;
typical of regional construction by German settlers.

Private.

National Historic Landmark.

* * *

SC235 BLOCKER HOUSE

Edgefield, SC   29824

1775

Area's oldest occupied house. Built as overseer's
house by Prussian immigrant Michael Blocker.

Private.

* * *

TX236 CASTROVILLE HISTORIC DISTRICT

Castroville, TX   78009

19th century

District composed of residences, commercial buildings,
churches, and courthouse; buildings are often of
limestone or Fachwerk, with some log structures.
Community founded in 1840's by immigrants from Rhine
Valley, encouraged to settle here by Henri Castro,
French impresario; over 700 inhabitants by 1847; town
has retained distinctive Alsatian character.

Multiple public/private.

Historic American Buildings Survey.

* * *

Pennsylvania-Texas (Sites)

TX237 FREDERICKSBURG HISTORIC DISTRICT

Fredericksburg, TX 78624

mid-late 19th century

Contains residential architecture typically featuring 1½-story gabled houses of limestone, log, or <u>Fachwerk</u> construction; and a few small "Sunday houses," or town residences used by the area's farmers on weekends. Town grew around predominantly German settlement established in 1846; early town center was the <u>Vereins-kirche</u>, an octagonal church demolished in 1896 and reconstructed near original site in 1930.

Multiple public/private.

Cf. PIONEER MEMORIAL MUSEUM, TX121.

* * *

TX238 MASON HISTORIC DISTRICT

U. S. Route 87 & State Route 29
Mason, TX 76856

19th-early 20th century

District comprised of commercial and residential struc-tures, with variety of treatment including many stone buildings, false-fronted frame structures, pressed tin facades, a <u>Fachwerk</u> house, etc. Town developed with mostly German settlers, following founding of nearby Fort Mason.

Multiple public/private.

Cf. MASON COUNTY MUSEUM, TX123.

* * *

TX239 FIRST PROTESTANT CHURCH (UNITED CHURCH OF CHRIST)

296 South Seguin Street
New Braunfels, TX 78130

Built to house area's German congregation.

Private.

* * *

TX240 STEPHEN KLEIN HOUSE

131 Seguin Street
New Braunfels, TX 78130

1846

<u>Fachwerk</u>, stuccoed 1-story house. Typical of early German construction in America.

Private; not accessible to the public.

* * *

Texas (Sites)

TX241 LINDHEIMER HOUSE

    489 Comal Avenue
    New Braunfels, TX   78130

    ca. 1852

    <u>Fachwerk</u>, stuccoed, 1½-story house. Home of botanist
    Ferdinand Lindheimer, who fought in the war for Texas
    Independence and who started printing a newspaper in
    1852 at the rear of the house.

    Private.

    Historic American Buildings Survey.

* * *

TX242 KING WILLIAM HISTORIC DISTRICT

    San Antonio, TX

    late-19th century

    Residential district of imposing homes adjacent to
    downtown. Area established primarily by prosperous
    German businessmen in mid-late 19th century.

    Multiple private.

    Historic American Buildings Survey.

* * *

TX243 LA VILLITA HISTORIC DISTRICT

    San Antonio, TX

    18th-20th centuries

    Residential district adjacent to downtown includes 27
    significant buildings; European-type quarter probably
    inhabited by ca. 1768, established by Spanish immi-
    grants on land originally belonging to the Alamo;
    German immigrants arrived in 1840's; later Swiss and
    French peoples settled here also.

    Multiple public/private.

    Historic American Buildings Survey.

* * *

TX244 MENGER SOAP WORKS

    400 block of North Laredo Street
    San Antonio, TX   78207

    ca. 1850

    Only antebellum industrial building in Texas. Possibly
    the first soap factory in the Southwest, founded by
    German immigrant Simon Menger; operated until ca. 1915.

    Private.

* * *

Texas (Sites)

TX245 OLD LONE STAR BREWERY

110-116 Jones Avenue
San Antonio, TX 78215

1895-1904

Brewery opened 1884; expanded under direction of
Adolphus Busch of Anheuser-Busch; design adapted to
varied needs of brewery process, built with fireproof
construction techniques; rear semi-enclosed park
provided rest and recreation place for employees and
visitors.

Private.

* * *

VA246 TUNKER HOUSE (YOUNT-ZIGLER HOUSE)

State Route 786 & 42
Broadway, VA 22815

ca. 1798

Main room of brick house used for religious services
until 1830 by the German Baptists (or Tunker Brethren).

Private; not accessible to the public.

* * *

VA247 JOHN K. BERRY FARM

Harrisonburg, VA 22801

1838-1839

Farm complex containing numerous buildings such as
barn, loom house, and springhouse arranged around limestone farmhouse. Scots-Irish and German construction
techniques. Following tradition, one wing served as
meeting room for large congregation of Mennonites.

Private.

* * *

VA248 NEW MARKET HISTORIC DISTRICT

Jct. U. S. 11 & 211
New Market, VA 22844

18th-19th centuries

Linear town along old Valley Pike; contains primarily
two-story frame and brick gabled residential, commercial, and religious structures, most constructed early-
mid 19th century. Town laid out in 1785, became an
active mercantile center in early-19th century. Prominent among many German inhabitants was Ambrose Henkel,
founder of the Henkel Press, the oldest Lutheran
Press in America (1806).

Multiple public/private.

Historic American Buildings Survey.

                        * * *   Texas-Virginia (Sites)

VA249 FORT PHILIP LONG

      Stanley, VA   22851

      18th-19th centuries

      Remains of building complex consisting of an under-
      ground fort, now partially exposed, connected by a
      tunnel to a 1½-story stone gabled house; brick dwelling;
      slave quarters. Built by descendant of German immi-
      grant who settled here during German migration into
      area in late 1720's and early 1730's. Example of
      fortifications constructed by area families during and
      after the French and Indian War.

      Private.

* * *

WI250 VOLKSFREUND BUILDING

      200 East College Avenue
      Appleton, WI   54911

      1880's

      Housed offices of the Appleton Volksfreund, state's
      second largest 19th-century foreign language publica-
      tion, with 6,000 subscribers in 1895.

      Private.

* * *

WI251 KOEPSEL HOUSE

      Eagle, WI   53119

      ca. 1860

      Half-timber frame, brick nogging. One of state's most
      impressive examples of the half-timber houses built by
      German immigrants.

      State-owned; not accessible to the public.

      Historic American Buildings Survey.

      Cf. OLD WORLD WISCONSIN, WI134.

* * *

WI252 CHRISTIAN TURCK HOUSE

      Eagle, WI   53119

      ca. 1830

      One of few Wisconsin houses reflec... ... ...cal German
      Blockbau construction.

      State-owned.

      Historic American Buildings Survey.

      Cf. OLD WORKD WISCONSIN, WI134.

* * *

Virginia-Wisconsin (Sites)

WI253 OLD ST. MARY'S CHURCH

    844 North Broadway
    Milwaukee, WI   53202

    1846-1847

    City's oldest surviving church; built for community's
    first German-speaking Roman Catholic parish.

    Private.

    Historic American Buildings Survey.

* * *

WI254 PABST THEATER

    144 East Wells Street
    Milwaukee, WI   53202

    1895

    Otto Straack, architect. Built for German beer magnate
    Frederick Pabst; opened as German theater; important
    element in city's cultural life.

    Municipal.

    Historic American Buildings Survey.

* * *

WI255 FRIEDERICH KOHLMANN HOUSE

    Springfield Corners, WI   53176

    1867

    Stone farmhouse typical of construction by area's
    German immigrants.

    Private; not accessible to the public.

* * *

Chapter III:

SELECTED LIST
OF EUROPEAN SOURCES

D256   ALTONAER MUSEUM (Altona Museum)

2000 Hamburg-Altona 50
  Museumstrasse 23
Federal Republic of Germany

Mariners' museum of Northern Germany. Shipping and
navigation; ship-models; folklife; folk art; costumes,
toys.

* * *

D257   BREMER STAATSARCHIV (State Archive of Bremen)

2800 Bremen
  Präsident-Kennedy-Platz 1
Federal Republic of Germany

Bibliographic and pictorial materials and manuscripts
relating to the history of Bremen and Bremerhafen.
Emigrants' newspapers and other publications, with
excellent engravings and photographs of the emigration
process.

* * *

D258   DEUTSCHES SCHIFFAHRTSMUSEUM (German Museum of Shipping
        and Navigation)

2850 Bremerhafen
  Georgstrasse 19
Federal Republic of Germany

History of German shipping and navigation. Special
exhibit on emigration from Bremerhafen mounted in 1975.

* * *

D259   DEUTSCHES VOLKSLIEDARCHIV (German Library and Museum of
       Folksong)

       7800 Freiburg im Breisgau
         Silberbachstrasse 13
       Federal Republic of Germany

       Collections illustrating development of German folksong
       and folkdance. Of special interest are sheet music and
       recordings of Auswanderlieder (songs of emigrants),
       some of which were collected in Kansas.

                              * * *

D260   FOCKE-MUSEUM

       2800 Bremen
         Schwachauser-Heerstrasse 240
       Federal Republic of Germany

       Local folklore, shipping. Emigration documents (in
       picture archive) include advertising media, pictures
       of emigrant hotels, tickets, correspondence between
       emigrants and agents.

                              * * *

D261   GERMANISCHES NATIONALMUSEUM (German National Museum)

       8500 Nürnberg
         Kornmarkt 1
       Federal Republic of Germany

       German arts and cultural history: crafts, peasant
       furniture, costumes, musical instruments, toys,
       weapons, hunting equipment.

                              * * *

DDR   HEIMATMUSEUM "ALT-HERRNHUTER-STUBEN" ("Alt-Herrnhuter-
262   Stube" Regional Museum)

       DDR-8709 Herrnhut
         Löbauerstrasse 18
       German Democratic Republic

       Herrnhut was the mother colony of Moravian settlements
       in the United States and Canada. Collections are
       housed in an 18th-century townhouse.

                              * * *

D263   HEIMATSTELLE PFALZ (Palatine Regional Museum)

       6750 Kaiserslautern
         Benzinoring 6
       Federal Republic of Germany

       Documents, artifacts, and photographs relating to
       Palatine life and emigration.

                              * * *

F264   MUSÉE ALSACIEN (Alsatian Museum)

25 Quai Saint-Nicolas
F-67000 Strasbourg
France

Regional museum of Alsace.   Folk art, furniture,
costumes; wine industry.

* * *

L265   MUSÉES DE L'ÉTAT (Luxembourg State Museum)

Marché aux Poissons
Luxembourg
Luxembourg

General museum of Luxembourg; history, folklife;
decorative arts.

* * *

D266   MUSEUM FÜR HAMBURGISCHE GESCHICHTE (Museum of the
History of Hamburg)

2000 Hamburg
  Holstenwall 24
Federal Republic of Germany

History of Hamburg: guilds, trade, transport (especially railways and shipping); folklife; ship-models
and other articles relating to the emigration process.

* * *

A267   ÖSTERREICHISCHES FREILICHTMUSEUM (Austrian Open-Air
Museum)

A-8114 Stübing bei Graz
Austria

Open-air museum of Austrian folklife.

* * *

A268   ÖSTERREICHISCHES MUSEUM FÜR VOLKSKUNDE (Austrian
Folklife Museum)

A-1010 Wien
  Laudongasse 19
Austria

Museum of Austrian folklife.

* * *

CH269 SCHWEIZERISCHES LANDESMUSEUM (Swiss National Museum)

CH-8023 Zürich
  Museumstrasse 2
  Postfach 2760
Switzerland

General museum of Swiss culture and history.

* * *

CH270 SCHWEIZERISCHES MUSEUM FÜR VOLKSKUNDE, in the
       Museum für Völkerkunde (Swiss Folklife Museum, in the
       Anthropological Museum)

       CH-4000 Basel
         Augustinergasse
       Switzerland

       Regional museum of Swiss folk culture.

                            * * *

D271   THEODOR-ZINK MUSEUM

       6750 Kaiserslautern
         Rathaus
       Federal Republic of Germany

       Museum of the folklife of the Palatinate.

                            * * *

APPENDIX:
CULTURAL ATTACHES
IN WASHINGTON
AND OTTAWA

Austria

Press Counselor
Embassy of Austria
2343 Massachusetts Avenue NW
Washington, DC 20008
(202) 483-4474

Embassy of Austria
445 Wilbrod Street
Ottawa K1N 6M7
(613) 235-5521 or 235-5546

East Germany

Third Secretary for Cultural Affairs
Embassy of the German Democratic Republic
1717 Massachusetts Avenue NW
Washington, DC 20036
(202) 232-3134

West Germany

Attaché for Cultural Affairs
Embassy of the Federal Republic of Germany
4645 Reservoir Road NW
Washington, DC 20007
(202) 331-3000

West Germany, cont.

Embassy of the Federal Republic of Germany
1 Waverly Street
Ottawa K2P OT8
(613) 232-1101

Luxembourg

Attaché
Embassy of Luxembourg
2200 Massachusetts Avenue NW
Washington, DC 20008
(202) 265-4171

Switzerland

Counselor for Cultural Affairs
Embassy of Switzerland
2900 Cathedral Avenue NW
Washington, DC 20008
(202) 462-1811

Embassy of Switzerland
5 Marlborough Avenue
Ottawa K1N 8E6
(613) 235-1837

BIBLIOGRAPHY

History

Arndt, Karl J. R. George Rapp's Harmony Society,
1785-1847. Philadelphia: University of Pennsylvania Press,
1965.

Barry, Colman. The Catholic Church and German Americans.
Milwaukee: Bruce, 1953.

Cunz, Dieter. The Maryland Germans: A History.
Princeton: Princeton University Press, 1948.

Epp, Frank H. Mennonites in Canada, 1786-1920: The
History of a Separate People. Toronto: Macmillan of Canada,
1974.

Faust, Albert. The German Element in the United States.
New edition. New York: Steuben Society of America, 1927.

Fleming, Donald and Bernard Bailyn. The Intellectual
Migration: Europe and America, 1930-60. Cambridge, Mass.:
Harvard University Press, 1969.

Furer, Howard B., comp. and ed. The Germans in America,
1607-1970: A Chronology and Fact Book. Ethnic Chronology
Series, no. 8. Dobbs Ferry, N.Y.: Oceana Publications,
1973.

Gingerich, Orland. The Amish of Canada. Waterloo:
Conrad Press, 1972.

Hamilton, J. Taylor and Kenneth Hamilton. History of the
Moravian Church: The Renewed Unitas Fratrum, 1722-1957.
Bethlehem: Moravian Church in America, 1967.

Hansen, Marcus Lee. The Atlantic Migration, 1607-1860:
A History of the Continuing Settlement of the United States.
Cambridge, Mass.: Harvard University Press, 1940.

Hawgood, John A. The Tragedy of German-America. New
York: G. P. Putnam's Sons, 1940.

Hostetler, John A. Amish Society. Baltimore: The
Johns Hopkins University Press, 1963.

Hostetler, John A. Hutterite Society. Baltimore: The
Johns Hopkins University Press, 1974.

Hostetler, John A. Mennonite Life. Scottdale, Pa.:
Herald, 1954.

Jordan, Terry. German Seed in Texas Soil: Immigrant
Farmers in Nineteenth Century Texas. Austin: University of
Texas Press, 1966.

Rippley, La Vern. The German-Americans. Boston:
Twayne Publishers, 1976.

Roueché, Berton. "Schoenheit Muss Leiden." The New
Yorker, February 28, 1977, pp. 37-50. (A Profile of
Hermann, Missouri)

Rush, Benjamin. An Account of the Manners of the German
Inhabitants of Pennsylvania. Philadelphia: S. P. Town,
1875. (Originally written in 1789)

Schelbert, Leo. New Glarus 1845-1970: The Making of a
Swiss American Town. Glarus: Verlag Tschudi, 1970.

Stumpp, Karl. The German Russians. New York: Atlantic
Forum, 1967.

Walker, Mack. Germany and the Emigration, 1816-1885.
Cambridge, Mass.: Harvard University Press, 1964.

Weinlick, John R. The Moravian Church in Canada.
Winston-Salem: The Provincial Women's Board of the Southern
Province, 1966.

Wentz, Abdel. A Basic History of Lutheranism in America.
Philadelphia: Muhlenberg Press, 1950.

Wittke, Carl. The Forty-Eighters: Political Refugees
of the German Revolution of 1848. New York: Columbia
University Press, 1950.

Wood, Ralph, ed. The Pennsylvania Germans. Princeton:
Princeton University Press, 1942.

Wust, Klaus. The Virginia Germans. Charlottesville:
University of Virginia Press, 1969.

Material Culture

America Through the Eyes of German Immigrant Painters.
Boston: Goethe Institute Boston, 1976.

Ames, Kenneth L. Beyond Necessity: Art in the Folk
Tradition. Winterthur: The Winterthur Museum, 1977.

Bivins, John. The Moravian Potters in North Carolina.
Chapel Hill: University of North Carolina Press, 1972.

Christensen, Erwin O. The Index of American Design.
New York: Macmillan Company, 1950.

Concepts of the Bauhaus: The Busch-Reisinger Museum
Collection. Cambridge, Mass.: Harvard College, 1971.

Dornbusch, Charles. Pennsylvania German Barns.
Allentown, Pa.: Schlechters, 1958.

Gehret, Ellen J. and Alan G. Keyser. The Homespun
Textile Tradition of the Pennsylvania Germans. Harrisburg:
Pennsylvania Historical & Museum Commission, 1976.

Lichten, Frances. Folk Art of Rural Pennsylvania.
New York: Scribners, 1963.

Murtagh, William J. Moravian Architecture and Town
Planning; Bethlehem, Pennsylvania, and Other Eighteenth-
Century American Settlements. Chapel Hill: University of
North Carolina Press, 1967.

Perrin, Richard. Historic Wisconsin Buildings: A Survey
of Pioneer Architecture, 1835-70. Milwaukee: Milwaukee
Public Museum, 1962.

Taylor, Lonn and David B. Warren. Texas Furniture: The
Cabinetmakers and Their Work, 1840-1880. Austin: University
of Texas Press, 1975.

Van Ravensway, Charles. The Arts and Architecture
of German Settlements in Missouri: A Survey of a Vanishing
Culture. Columbia, Mo.: University of Missouri Press, 1977.

Yoder, Don, Vernon S. Gunnion, and Carroll J. Hopf.
Pennsylvania German Fraktur and Color Drawings. Lancaster:
Landis Valley Associates, 1969.

Reference Works

    Ash, Lee. Subject Collections. New York: R. R. Bowker,
1967.

    Chenhall, Robert G. Nomenclature for Museum Cataloging:
A System for Classifying Man-Made Objects. Nashville:
American Association for State and Local History, 1978.

    Directory of Historical Societies and Agencies in the
United States and Canada. Tenth Edition. Nashville:
American Association for State and Local History, 1975.

    Directory of Museums, Art Galleries and Related Institu-
tions, 1972. Ottawa: Information Canada, 1973.

    Encyclopedia of Associations. Tenth Edition. Detroit:
Gale Research, 1976.

    Hudson, Kenneth and Ann Nicholls, eds. The Directory
of World Museums. New York: Columbia University Press,
1975.

    Keresztesi, Michael and Gary R. Cocozzoli. German-
American History and Life: A Guide to Information Sources.
Detroit: Gale Research, 1979.

    Kloss, Heinz. Atlas of German-American Settlements.
Marburg: N. G. Elwert, 1974.

    Markotic, Vladimir, comp. and ed. Ethnic Directory of
Canada. Calgary: Western Publishers, 1976.

    The National Register of Historic Places, 1976.
Washington, D. C.: U. S. Department of the Interior, 1976.

    The Official Museum Directory, 1978-79. Washington,
D. C.: American Association of Museums, 1978.

    Picture Sources III: Collections of Prints and
Photographs in the United States and Canada. New York:
Special Libraries Association, 1975.

    Shaw, Renata V. Picture Searching: Techniques and
Tools. New York: Special Libraries Association, 1973.

    Tolzmann, Don Heinrich. German-Americana: A Bibliography.
Metuchen, N. J.: The Scarecrow Press, 1975.

    Wasserman, Paul and Jean Morgan, eds. Ethnic Information
Sources of the United States. Detroit: Gale Research, 1976.

Wynar, Lubomyr R. Encyclopedic Directory of Ethnic
Organizations in the United States. Littleton, Colo.:
Libraries Unlimited, Inc., 1975.

Wynar, Lubomyr and Lois Buttlar, eds. Guide to Ethnic
Museums, Libraries and Archives in the United States.
Kent, O.: Center for Ethnic Publications, 1978.

NAME INDEX

William W. Badgley Historical Museum	NY60
Bauhaus Study Archive	MA30
John K. Beery Farm	VA247
Beggarstown School	PA227
H. H. Bennett Studio, Inc.	WI142
Berks County, Historical Society of	PA105
Bethabara, Historic	NC63
Bethabara Moravian Church	NC201
Bethel College	KS25
	KS26
Bethel Historic District	MO183
Bethlehem Historic District	PA212
Bethlehem, Historic, Inc.	PA80
Bettman Archive, Inc.	NY52
Black Creek Pioneer Village	ON149
Black Star Publishing Company, Inc.	NY53
Blocker House	SC235
Blue Earth County Historical Society Museum	MN34
Blue Ridge Farm Museum	VA130
Borgmann Mill	MO187
Michael Braun House	NC197
Bremer Staatsarchiv	D257
Brendle Farms	PA230
Thomas R. Brendle Memorial Library and Museum	PA107
Bridgewater College	VA129
Brown Brothers Stock Photos	PA109
Brown County Historical Society	MN35
Bucks County Historical Society	PA84
Buffalo and Erie County Historical Society	NY48
J. R. Burdick Collection	NY55
Busch-Reisinger Museum	MA30
California Historical Society	CA4
Carroll County Farm Museum	MD28
Carver County Historical Society, Inc.	MN38
Castroville Historic District	TX236
Center for Mennonite Brethren Studies	CA2
Chicago Historical Society	IL10
Philip Christman House	PA211

Keim Homestead	PA223
Annie S. Kemerer Museum	PA81
Kiesling House	MN178
King William Historic District	TX242
Klein Meetinghouse	PA218
Stephen Klein House	TX240
Kluge House	MT190
Knurr Log House	PA216
Koepsel House	WI251
Friederich Kohlmann House	WI255
Dielman Kolb Homestead	PA221
Charles Krug Winery	CA154
Lancaster County Historical Society	PA91
Lancaster Mennonite Conference Historical Society	PA90 PA92
Landis Valley, Pennsylvania Farm Museum of	PA93
Arne B. Larson Collection of Musical Instruments and Library	SD118
La Villita Historic District	TX243
Lehigh County Historical Society	PA78
Library of Congress	DC7
Library of Vehicles	CA3
Lindheimer House	TX241
Lititz Moravian Congregation	PA96
Llano County Historical Museum	TX122
Peter Loewen Adobe House	KS23
Long Meadow Farm	PA233
Luxembourg State Museum	L265
McPherson Museum	KS24
Manitoba Mennonite Historical Society	MB143
Markham District Historical Museum	ON148
Maryland Historical Society	MD27
Mason County Museum	TX123
Mason Historic District	TX238
Witwe Mehwaldt House	NY47
Melges Bakery	MN179
Menger Soap Works	TX244
Mennonite Church, Archives of the	IN13

GENERAL INDEX

The terms used in this index may be broken down into three categories: one refers to events in German-American history (European roots, immigration process, places of settlement); a second group consists of subjects of historical photographs (organizations, street scenes, portraits); the third and largest group lists articles of material culture (furniture, tools, buildings).

The terms applied to the last group are mostly drawn from Robert G. Chenhall's Nomenclature for Museum Cataloging. Terms relevant or unique to German-Americana have been added where needed. The subject categories are broad. The purpose of this book has been to give an overview of material culture of German-speaking people in the United States and Canada, and to facilitate more detailed research in specific areas.

Little material on known German-American artists has been included. The area of painting has been well covered by the exhibit, "America Through the Eyes of German Immigrant Painters," created by the Goethe Institute, Boston, in 1975. The Institute's excellent catalog by the same title (see bibliography) would be very useful to researchers interested in this subject. Two major Bauhaus repositories (The Museum of Modern Art and The Busch-Reisinger Museum) have been described, and they are good starting points for further research in this area. The field of Pennsylvania German decorative arts is very well-documented. In this area only broad terms such as "furniture" and "fractur" are given in the index.

The entries for museum collections (CA1-SK152), National Register sites (CA153-WI255), and European sources (D256-D271) are arranged in numerical order. Letter codes indicating state, province or country have been prefixed to each entry number to help the user discern the geographical

location of the collection or site. These letter codes
should be ignored, however, when the user is trying to find
an entry cited in the index. The letter codes are explained
below.

        Entry numbers marked with an asterisk indicate large
or otherwise outstanding collections.

EXPLANATION OF LETTER CODES

California	CA	Texas	TX
Connecticut	CT	Virginia	VA
Delaware	DE	Wisconsin	WI
Washington, D. C.	DC		
Georgia	GA		
Illinois	IL		
Indiana	IN		
Iowa	IA	Manitoba	MB
Kansas	KS	Nova Scotia	NS
Maine	ME	Ontario	ON
Maryland	MD	Saskatchewan	SK
Massachusetts	MA		
Michigan	MI		
Minnesota	MN		
Missouri	MO		
Montana	MT	Austria	A
Nebraska	NE	France	F
New Jersey	NJ	Germany, East	DDR
New Mexico	NM	Germany, West	D
New York	NY	Luxembourg	L
North Carolina	NC	Switzerland	CH
North Dakota	ND		
Ohio	OH		
Oregon	OR		
Pennsylvania	PA		
South Carolina	SC		
South Dakota	SD		

Baskets, IA19

Bauhaus, MA30*, NY56

Bavarian, MI33

Bedding, DE6, DC9, IN15,
  IN16, IA20, KS21, KS23,
  KS24, MD28, MI33, MN35,
  MO41, NE45, NE46, NY47,
  NY60, NC62, NC63, NC65,
  ND67, OH68, OH76, PA78,
  PA79, PA81, PA83, PA84,
  PA85, PA86, PA87, PA88,
  PA89, PA90, PA92, PA93,
  PA95, PA98, PA101*, PA103,
  PA104, PA105, PA106, PA110,
  PA111, PA113, PA114, SD115,
  TX119, TX121, TX122, TX123,
  TX124, TX125, VA129, WI134,
  WI137, WI138, WI140, MB143,
  NS144, ON145, ON146, ON148

Berczy, ON148

Bethel, Society of, MO183,
  MO184, OR209, OR210

Bethlehem, Pennsylvania,
  PA80, PA81, PA83, PA212,
  PA213, PA214, PA215

Bibles, IN15, MN34, NE46,
  OH73, PA86, PA100, PA107,
  VA129*, ON146, ON149, SK150

Blockbau, WI252

Blueprints, NY56, PA79, PA80,
  PA82, ON147

Brethren, Church of the,
  VA129

Brethren, United in Christ
  see: United Brethren in
           Christ

Brewery, MD170, MN180, MO188,
  TX245

Brewing equipment, WI137,
  MN180

Brewing industry, MO40,
  MO42*, NY48, NC63, OH69,
  OH71, OH72, WI135, WI137*,
  WI142, MD170, MN180

Broadsides, IL10, IN14,
  PA99*, WI135

Buffalo, New York, NY48

Building (actual structure)
  See also: Architecture
             Bakehouse/
                Bakeoven
             Bakery
             Bank
             Bank barn
             Bank house
             Barber shop
             Barn
             Blockbau
             Blueprints
             Brewery
             Building,
                recreational
             Church
             Cider mill
             Coop, chicken
             Corncrib
             Corpse house
             Corral
             Depot
             Dormitory
             Fachwerk
             Factory
             Farmstead
             Fort
             Granary
             Hospital
             Hotel
             House
             House, fruit-
                drying
             Icehouse
             Inn
             Kiln
             Kitchen
             Mill
             Outhouse
             Post office
             Print shop
             Pumphouse
             Reconstruction
             Restoration
             School
             Shed

Church (photographs and
    ephemera), MN35, MO42,
    NE46, NY58, OH71, PA99,
    PA102, TX127, WI142

Cider mill, IN15, OH73,
    PA108, ON149

Cincinnati, Ohio, OH69, OH206

Cinema, CA1, DC7, NY56, NY57

Cleveland, Ohio, OH71

Clocks (timekeeping equip-
    ment), DC9, MO42, PA81,
    PA83, PA89, PA101, PA103,
    SK152

Clothing, DE6, DC8, DC9,
    IL10, IN14, IN15, IN16,
    IN18, IA20, KS21, KS23,
    KS24, KS25, MD28, MI33,
    MN35, MO39, MO40, MO41,
    NE45, NE46, NY47, NY60,
    NC65, ND66, ND67, OH68,
    OH69, OH76, PA79, PA80,
    PA83, PA84, PA85, PA86,
    PA87, PA88, PA89, PA91,
    PA92, PA93, PA94, PA96,
    PA97, PA98, PA101, PA105,
    PA106, PA113, PA114, SD115,
    TX119, TX120, TX121, TX122,
    TX123, TX124, TX125, VA129,
    VA131, WI134, WI137, WI138,
    WI140, MB143, NS144, ON145,
    ON146, ON148, D256, D261,
    F264

Clubs
    See: Organizations & Clubs

Columbus, Ohio, OH207

Conestoga wagon, CA2, PA84,
    PA87, PA89, PA101, PA105,
    PA114, ON146

Containers, DC8, DC9, IN14,
    IN16, IN18, IA19*, KS21,
    KS23, KS25, MD28, MI33,
    MO41, NE45, NE46, NY47,
    NY60, NC63, NC65, ND67,
    OH68, PA78, PA79, PA82,
    PA84, PA86, PA87, PA89,
    PA92, PA93, PA95, PA96,

(Containers)
    PA97, PA98, PA101*, PA102,
    PA106, PA110, PA111, PA113,
    PA114, SD115, TX119, TX121,
    TX122, TX123, TX125, VA129,
    VA132, WI134, WI138, WI140,
    MB143, NS144, ON145, ON146

Coop, chicken, MD28, MN37,
    NE44, KS164

Corncrib, MD28, NC61, PA111

Corpse House, PA96

Corral, MT189

Dakotas
    See: North Dakota
          South Dakota

Decorative arts (meant in
    the narrow sense of objects
    which serve only a decora-
    tive function), CT5, DE6,
    DC8*, DC9, IN12, IN14,
    IN16, IN17, IA19, IA20,
    KS21, KS23, MD28, MA29,
    MI33, MO39, MO41, NE45,
    NY47, NY58, NC61, NC63,
    NC65, ND67, OH68, OH76,
    PA78, PA79, PA80, PA82,
    PA83, PA85, PA87, PA88,
    PA89, PA91, PA92, PA93,
    PA94, PA96, PA97, PA98,
    PA100, PA101, PA102, PA103,
    PA105, PA106, PA111, PA113,
    PA114, SD115, TX119, TX124,
    TX125, TX128, VA129, VA131,
    VA132, WI134, WI137, WI138,
    WI140, MB143, ON145, ON146,
    ON148, D156, F264, LX265

Depot, NE44

Dishes
    See: Food processing &
          service articles

Dolls
    See: Toys

Dormitory, IN17, MD28, NC65,
    OH76, PA86, PA96, TX125,
    NC204

Rhinelander, NC61, TX236

Russian-Germans
  See: Germans from Russia

Sacramento, California,
  CA153

St. Louis, Missouri, MO42,
  MO188

Salzburger, GA156

San Antonio, Texas, TX126,
  TX127, TX242, TX243, TX244,
  TX245

San Francisco, California,
  CA4

Saskatchewan, SK150, SK151,
  SK152

Saxon, MO39

Schoenbrunn, Ohio, OH72

Schoharie Valley, New York,
  NY59, NY60

School (actual structure),
  IA19, KS21, KS23, MN35,
  MN37, MO39, MO40, NE44,
  NC61, NC65, PA79, PA85,
  PA86, PA93, PA94, SD115,
  WI133, WI139, WI141, MB143,
  ON145, MI174, PA227, PA228

School (photographs and
  ephemera), CA4, MD27,
  MO42, TX127

Schwenkfelder, PA98

Shed, IA19, KS23, MD28, NE44,
  OH68, PA78, PA79, PA108,
  PA111, PA113, TX121, VA130,
  WI139, WI140, ON146, ON149,
  PA232

Shop (includes store), NE44,
  NC61, NC63, NC65, OH73,
  OH76, PA79, PA83, PA86,
  PA89, PA93, WI139, MB143,
  ON149, CA154, IA162, NC204

Silo, KS164

Slaughterhouse, ON149

Smithy, NE44, OH76, PA93,
  WI133, MB143, ON146

Smokehouse, MD28, MN37, PA111,
  TX121, WI133

South Carolina, SC235

South Dakota, NE46, SD115,
  SD116, SD117

Springhouse, MD28, PA80,
  PA111, VA247

Stable, PA86, CA153

Stoveplates, DC8, PA84*,
  PA97, PA103, PA113

Street scenes, CA4, NY48,
  PA99, WI141, WI142

Sty, ON149, KS164

Sunday house, TX121, TX127,
  TX237

Sutter's Mill, California,
  CA4

Swiss, IN12, OH68, PA107,
  PA108, WI139, PA230,
  CH269, CH270

Tannery, PA80

Tavern, NC65, PA114, IA160,
  NC203, PA228

Texas, KS26, TX119, TX120,
  TX121, TX122, TX123, TX124,
  TX125, TX126, TX127*,
  TX128, TX236, TX237, TX238,
  TX239, TX240, TX241, TX242,
  TX243, TX244, TX245

Textileworking tools, DC9,
  IN15, IN16, IN17, IN18,
  IA19, KS21, KS23, KS24,
  KS25, MD28, MI33, MN34,

ABOUT THE COMPILER

MARGARET HOBBIE is Director of the Consulting Program at the Regional Conference of Historical Agencies in Manlius, New York. Her special interests include German-American history and American folk culture.